My pulse is not what it used to be

My pulse is not what it used to be

The leadership challenges in health care

Irwin M. Rubin, PhD
President, The Temenos® Foundation

C. Raymond Fernandez, MD
Piedmont Medical Center & Piedmont Medical Care
Executive Vice President of Physician Practices
Piedmont Clinic – Chief Executive Officer & Chief Medical Officer

The TEMENOS® Foundation

First published 1991
by The Temenos® Foundation, 37 Kawananakoa PI, Honolulu, HI 96837

Typeset in Sabon

ISBN: 1-904235-17-4

Rubin, Irwin M. and Fernandez, C. Raymond

Dedication

Na kahuna lapa'au (Hawaiian): "Expert practitioners who cure illness"

THE PRACTICE OF medicine is in an unhealthy and costly state of disease. Suspicion and mistrust have infected the sacred nature of the doctor-patient relationship. As a result, the central issue facing the profession of medicine is "how we [doctors] will respond to the challenges of public accountability for quality: with anxiety, reluctance, and defensive action, or with confidence, enthusiasm, and a sense of pride...".[1]

This book is dedicated to the growing body of physicians in management, *na kahuna lapa'au*, whose patients needing quality care are organisations of providers. We hope that by reading its message, they will draw the experience, strength, and hope that they require to move forward with confidence, enthusiasm and pride. The success of their effort is vitally important, for at some point in our lives, we are all touched by the practice and business of medical care.

---

[1] Dr. Donald Berwick, "Measuring Health Care Quality", *Pediatrics in Review*, 10, no. 1 (July 1988), p. 16.

Acknowledgements

Irwin Rubin
Honolulu, March 1991

THIS BOOK IS intended to be a message of hope—massaging the heart and feeding the soul—as well as stimulating the mind and engaging the intellect of a badly beleaguered profession. Given that vision, it comes as little surprise that this final section has been harder for me to draft than any other. Letting go of a baby I've come to hold near and dear to my heart is (as Dr. Fernandez writes), emotionally painful.

I feel a parental sense of both incompleteness ("I know it could be better"), and pride ("I can't believe how it has grown"), as well as a sense of gratitude that mere words cannot convey. Bruce Fritch, Keith Korenchuk, Gail Fernandez, and Drs. Kevin Sullivan and John Benedum have generously added essential perspectives. In addition to writing his own insightful commentary, Dr. Henry Berman has functioned as an invisible co-author throughout. Without his emotional and substantive support, I might have taken the easier, softer way out upon occasion and settled for less from myself.

When my ego resistance to Henry's help remained firm, my trusted editors, first David Nelson and then Tracey Bennett, would rise to the challenge. Tracey, in particular, had the remarkable ability to hang in with me long enough so that I could finally let go and say what I meant.

When all else failed, standing beside me and getting through my ego's defensiveness, as she has done with love and care since the day we met, is my silent partner, best friend, and treasured wife, Nan Holmes.

Readers will be privileged to get to know and appreciate for themselves Dr. Ray Fernandez. There are qualities of the man that only face-to-face contact can provide. While this book is about Charles Ray Fernandez as a personality, it is a tribute to him that his motivation and commitment have, throughout, been in support of a principle. Treating people in the most humane way possible is a fact of life for Ray

Fernandez. Equally unshakeable is his faith in the fundamental goodness of our human nature.

Without Dr. Ray Fernandez and his profession and the principles they represent, this book, and the message of hope that it carries, would remain the mere vision of an idea. At some point in our lives we are all touched by the practice and business of medical care, and we all owe it a measure of grateful acknowledgement.

Acknowledgements to the second edition

The second edition of *My Pulse* has been significantly enriched by many, beginning with the Fraser family. The meat in between was provided by Nigel Edwards, Dr. Tim Wilson, Dr. Jeremiah Holleman, Jr., M.D., Mary Jane Kornacki, MS, and Jack Silversin, DMD, Dr.PH. Never one to leave any job unfinished, Dr. Fernandez opens his heart once again and revisits painful memories. To one and all, we owe a deep sense of gratitude and respect.

Contents

Forewords

Nigel Edwards
Policy Director, National Health Service Confederation, Great Britain

Dr. Tim Wilson
General Practitioner and Policy Analyst, Department of Health Strategy Unit, Great Britain

Editor's note: I have had the good fortune to share the ideas contained in the first edition of *My Pulse* with many committed health care professionals around the globe who struggle, within their own organisations, to deliver the highest levels of patient care possible. One very clear lesson has emerged from these opportunities. While the specifics of a particular organisation's or nation's supporting systems, structures, and procedures may vary considerably, there is one constant that transcends any and all boundaries and differences. Each and every health care encounter involves human beings coming in contact with one another.

As we shall see, for example, from the two pieces which follow, the challenges of maintaining this singular focus on the care of human beings—the *sine qua non* of the profession—are fundamentally no different in the nationalised health care environment of Great Britain [and, as I recently observed first hand in Sweden as well] than in the public and private sectors of the United States. Keeping in mind this simple premise—that people in need of care are people who, appropriately so, should not have to care about the details of the systems, structures, and procedures supporting that care—will, we hope, enable readers around the globe to draw lessons they can best adapt for their own specific use.

IT IS VERY EASY to assume that the problems experienced by NHS organisations are due to our unique circumstances. It is particularly popular at the moment to blame government, bad management or other characteristics that it is imagined are exclusive to the NHS. Many of the challenges we face are found in other health care systems, and although the Nalle Clinic was operating in another time and in a very different system, its growth and eventual failure illustrate lessons that apply in the UK.

The use of an extended metaphor draws our attention to a curious anomaly; despite the fact that health care has one of the most intelligent and educated workforces of any industry, it often appears largely unable to apply this collective ability to dealing with the difficulties it faces. Partly this seems to be the result of a reluctance to accept that clinical work is not separate from the political, economic and managerial domains that are an unavoidable part of modern life. It is no longer possible to pretend that a clinical decision does not have significant consequences for the rest of the system, for the allocation of resources and therefore, for the well being of the entire organisation.

Many leading doctors now argue that considering the resource implications of clinical decisions is an ethical imperative and that there is a duty to consider these when treating patients, but this view is far from universally accepted. In its more extreme forms, there is still a view that management is a baleful and unnecessary external intrusion imposed by government with the main purpose of frustrating high quality medicine. It is clear that we do not do enough to prepare the managers of health care to understand the ethos of medicine, or to help doctors understand the need to apply management principles to the practice of medicine.

Secondly, as the Nalle Clinic case study shows, many clinicians have difficulty understanding and engaging with the leaders of their organisations. The reverse is also true. Whilst there is a lot written about the importance of skilled leadership, the story of the Nalle Clinic (and many other struggling organisations) highlights how little attention is given to the equally challenging absence of skilled followers. Henry Mintzberg writes of the phenomenon of the disconnected hierarchy found in professional organisations where the front line professionals' practice is completely cut from the managerial level. Given the differences in approach, views on accountability and autonomy, team working, epistemology and attitudes to the resource consequences of clinical decisions between medicine and management, this lack of connection should not be too surprising.

One group that does not appear much in this story, but which might be important, are middle managers who are credible with clinicians and can help them contribute to the vision of the organisation and to engage them with it. We seem to have seriously neglected this group and since they are the main interface between management and clinical staff, this is, at least, unwise. Where these managers are effective, they provide invaluable translation services. Too often they are unhappily stressed in a sandwich between conflicting views and seen as a problem by both top managers and clinicians.

Many of the early signs of problems at the Nalle Clinic are also found in NHS organisations that run into difficulty. Lack of engagement with the objectives of the organisation, and the pursuit of personal or sectional objectives, is a common feature of organisations in the early stages of failure. In the UK, we increase the probability of this by a method of training and socialisation that fails to make many doctors feel part of an organisation. This is illustrated by the story of a Medical Director of a large trust (in existence for 3 years) who told me how, out of 13 applications for a distinction award (worth up to £40,000), more that half the consultants applying failed to correctly complete the name of their employing organisation. The Nalle Clinic seems to have suffered from overly hands-off management of clinical activity and poorly engaged clinicians. The incentive structure and the share option schemes seem to have helped to further distance the physicians from sharing in this. Although overly decentralised and disconnected management has been shown to be hazardous in the NHS, there are similar dangers associated with highly centralist and hierarchical approaches.

A third characteristic of failing organisations in the NHS is a lack of basic managerial processes and a failure to pay attention to key internal systems. This was also the case at the Nalle Clinic, and whilst they attributed part of their problem to the failure to invest in a new computer system, many organisations find that it is precisely the big project to install new computers, or replace a building, that is the last straw. This is often associated with a failure to really diagnose the underlying causes of the problems and to look for easy external solutions. In more extreme cases, there was a great deal of energy expended on denying the problems, blaming others and looking for external rescue, rather than facing up to the tough action required to reverse the decline.

External intervention can help, but the Nalle Clinic did not have an unbiased 'corporate parent' who could have kept an eye on its performance and perhaps intervened sooner. Unfortunately, in the NHS this type of intervention has not always been very helpful or timely. These intermediate bodies appeared to be aware that organisations were failing, but had done little other than ask for additional reports and information diverting even more time from the task of sorting out the problems. The problem for any 'parent' organisation is that whilst strategic overview is important, it does not necessarily place one in a good position for deciding what action needs to be taken down at the front line. Furthermore, there is a real danger of those higher up the system believing they know best, simply because they are higher up.

The most fatal problem—which also proved fatal to the Nalle Clinic —is a lack of the kind of leadership needed when a potentially lethal illness is looming at hand. Leadership is, of course, required at all points in the organisation but, in the case of those with significant problems operating in turbulent environments, it is particularly important that top leaders provide guidance, reinforce the message that the problems are real, that responsibility for addressing them is shared, and hold everyone to account for change. In contrast, the Nalle Clinic and the NHS organisations that we worked with that were failing seemed to have suffered from one final common feature. The absence of honest feedback or anyone prepared to hold up a mirror and to point out a truth that, whilst unacceptable, seems a universal insight in these situations: 'we have met the enemy, and he is us'.

Failing organisations, as a consequence, almost always act to completely change the top management team. Whilst this may, at times be necessary, lopping off the top of weed and leaving the roots will not solve the longer term problem. But if, like at the Nalle Clinic and other similar NHS organisations, there is not a realisation of what the causal problems [versus easily visible symptoms] are and the steps that are required, it is very likely that the organisation will not get the leaders willing and able to take this action.

Whilst some organisations fail because of a temporary lapse in systems or poor management which are relatively easy to correct, there is a second group whose failure is attributable to more fundamental cultural problems. These eat up and spit out chief executives and medical directors, they suffer years of poor performance and false dawns, and they recruit more and more staff who fit the dysfunctional culture.

The Nalle Clinic story reminds us that for these 'chronically ill' organisations, we need more patience and courage to take decisions that many will find difficult to live with. In some cases no option remains, and if the patient won't modify their behaviour, there can only be one outcome.

Nigel Edwards

'Y PULSE IS NOT WHAT IT USED TO BE' is a unique book. It offers the reader a privileged insight into the life of a health care organisation. You could, all too easily, dismiss this book because of its cultural context. For those of you who do not come from the United States, you may need some convincing that it has any relevance to you. For those of us brought up on cricket and real football (okay soccer) the sporting metaphors with their references to baseball, American football, and basketball hardly count as proper sport, more periods of activity interspersed with messages from "our sponsor". But enough poking fun at our American cousins, because this book's importance transcends hurdles relating to the Atlantic gulf.

In the UK especially, the physician or doctor CEO is a rare beast, just now being spotted in the swamplands of Primary Care Trusts. In that context, the compelling story of Dr. Raymond Fernandez will be alien to many of you. But don't give up. For the larger number of leaders who were previously nurses, the notion of the organisation as a living body will be easy to comprehend. And, for those without a clinical background, personal experience and insight will soon help you appreciate why this book works at so many levels. This book is for anyone involved in the running of health care organisations. The fact that the central player, Dr Fernandez, is a doctor allows us a helpful perspective, but does not mean this book has no relevance to non-doctors.

"But," you continue to protest, "UK health care is different; we do not have organisations like the Nalle Clinic." True, but we are talking about health care in a time of change and the US is not alone in that. The Nalle Clinic has many characteristics in common with what we do. In Germany, health care reform is looking at the way in which a gate-keeping function can be introduced. How will this affect the way health care works and operates? Is it going to have profound effects on the culture of health care? This is not like the simple addition of a new exhaust to a car, this is changing the way people, patients, and caregivers behave. Canada and Australia are concentrating on strengthening primary care. You cannot change a fundamental part of a system without major consequences, any more than you can operate on part of the body and expect the rest to behave as if nothing has happened. So, as we all go through transformations in health care, we can understand how this book applies to our own countries; the environmental changes experienced by the Nalle Clinic are no different to our own.

The UK is going through a period of enormous change within which runs deep cultural issues. For instance, the consultant contract, so overwhelmingly, and apparently surprisingly, rejected, is indicative of the deep mistrust between managers and doctors. This problem, high-lighted in the theme issue of the *British Medical Journal* (*BMJ*, 21st March 2003), shows that there is a deep dis-ease within the body of the NHS; not resistant to treatment but impossible to isolate from the rest of the NHS corporate. As Irv Rubin would tell us, "to ignore this festering staff infection is as dangerous as ignoring a festering staph infection."

Then why is this book important, why do I commend it to you?

First, we must recognise the living breathing nature of organisations. We read of the Stage I organisation growing and developing and feeling the pains of change, just as we remember our spotty faced adolescence when no one understood us. Each and every part is connected. The Nalle Clinic shows us what happens when we change one part, the other parts change. As the structures were altered, as surely as if the very skeleton of the body were altered, so the organisation felt the pains. As a patient's conditions wax and wane, so do the fortunes of organisations. If a doctor has ever made the "wrong" decision, or been fooled into a course of action by misleading symptoms, then so have the "attending" leaders in health care.

Second, just as learning from a clinical case review, significant event audit, or reflective practice helps us understand how we can better care for patients, so this "grand round" of the ultimately fatal case of the Nalle Clinic helps us learn. The narrative brings depth. Just as on the "grand round" clinical experts are able to tell us from the end of the patient bed the differential diagnoses and possible solutions, so this book takes us through the same process. We learn from differing per-spectives the multiple truths behind what happens in a disease process. One of the great strengths of this book are these multiple shared per-spectives from the contributing authors. The glimpse from every angle deepens and broadens our understanding of what happens in organisa-tions. Sometimes the descriptions appear contradictory, but each one is in its own right true. The contradiction is itself the truth. Fortunately for the reader, this book takes us through to the final autopsy of the Nalle Clinic, once a living breathing human organism. The value of the post-mortem in the medical world is well recognised, but how often do we get such an objective insight in the organisational world?

Third, as this book illustrates, how we behave within an organisation affects that organisation as surely as when we behave badly with a friend or colleague. Disruptive behaviour is common; in a survey of 2500 nurses, *only 2% had not* recently witnessed an episode of bad behaviour by medical colleagues. This book gives us insight into the effect this has. The book describes how the organisational equivalent of an x-ray is performed that gives some idea whether the espoused culture and real culture match. Is this an investigation that your own organisation needs?

Fourth, Rubin describes different stages any organisation might be in. Sadly, many in the NHS appear to be stuck in Stage I, perhaps because of their novelty, or because they are truly stuck. However, we are all aware of Stage II organisations and have exciting glimpses of Stage III. By seeing what happened at the Nalle Clinic, and then reflecting on "the quality of the journey" that our own organisations are on, we might understand better what is needed. For me personally, a core element of the book was the behavioural survey and its impact. Those of you who have read other works by Rubin will know that he strongly advocates the active management of behaviour as a key to changing culture. Behaviour alters attitudes, and attitude change might just alter more deeply held assumptions.

Lastly, just as those in health care are concerned with curing and healing, this book reminds us that those running a health care organisation need to remember the importance of caring and healing for the organisation, and the people within it. Irwin Rubin, Raymond Fernandez, and their co-authors have allowed us a view into a private world—the inner running of a health care organisation in transition. Not just a view of what happened in the meetings and conversations between people, but how they felt about it, what it meant to them.

My copy of this book is now full of annotations and folded page corners, a sure sign that I need to go back and reflect. For me, this book is full of these moments, as a partly obscured thought I had was clarified by the authors' perception or observation.

Dr. Tim Wilson

Case presentation

Medical record

Patient's name: The Nalle Clinic
Attending physician: Raymond Fernandez, MD, CEO
Chief complaint: Increasing overhead, trouble making decisions, poor morale
Presenting illness:

Editor's note to second edition: The fact that the Patient expired suddenly necessitated a detailed Autopsy. The last section of this edition contains that Autopsy Report.

THIS 70-YEAR-OLD multi-speciality clinic with nearly 80 physicians is located in a medium-sized southern city. From its inception, it has enjoyed progressive growth and an excellent regional reputation as a quality medical provider, notably of speciality care. More recently, it has expanded its primary care base. For years it had an extremely low rate of physician attrition. It was quite financially successful through the 1970s.

The Clinic's home city of Charlotte, North Carolina, has grown steadily. The physician community doubled between 1985 and 1990. Local hospitals expanded and began competing with one another and with physician groups. In 1984 HMOs (a Health Maintenance Organisation where patients can get all their health care for a fixed yearly premium) entered the community, and in only five years, expanded from zero to fifteen percent penetration. As these competitors began to market physicians' services, then competition and advertising, unheard of ten years previously, became standard.

Several speciality groups left the Clinic, including the entire nephrology and cardiology sections and major components of the orthopaedic and gastroenterology sections. Hiring high-earning subspecialists became quite difficult. Small niche groups were enjoying more financial

1

success in the community than this large multi-speciality group. Members began to question the compensation formula that had served the Clinic for 60 years. This formula, based on production, consisted of an equal-percentage contribution by all physicians. Some began to advocate cost accounting with its appealing variable contribution to overhead. Over a five-year period, two separate committees wrestled with a new compensation formula, but neither committee could get a new formula accepted.

Between 1985 and 1990 the Clinic changed its expensive computer system twice. Physicians grumbled more and more about reports from the data processing department, and eventually they began to disbelieve most reports. The percentage that physicians recognised of their billings continued to decline, as did the collection percentage. Although all physicians demanded "better management", their disdain for bureaucracy and administration intensified. Physicians did not volunteer to serve on the Board of Directors. Rather, like Monday morning quarterbacks, many knew exactly what plays should have been called. Few seemed willing to leave their seats on the 50-yard line and join the battle on the astro-turf.

Past medical history

In spite of escalating problems, the Clinic recorded numerous successes. It re-obtained three-year accreditation from the AAAHC. The Clinic's HMO quickly grew to 35,000 members, the most successful in the region. Over the most recent five-year period, the Clinic added three new satellites; began a seven-day, extended-hour, acute-care facility; dedicated a CT scanner; initiated a women's speciality centre with five physicians; and hired a marketing director. The number of patient visits continued to rise. In 1980 the Clinic introduced the role of medical director, and four years later, it established the role of CEO. On the level of national successes, a member of the Clinic has served as the President of the American Group Practice Association. Another of the Clinic's members went on to serve as President of the American Academy of Medical Directors.

In spite of many signs of good health, and in spite of improvements in the physicians' benefit package, the Clinic's debt load skyrocketed.

Review of systems

Managerial

The Clinic recognised that one person could not handle the administrative load. Previously, only one lay administrator had been responsible for the whole Clinic. The Clinic replaced this arrangement with a physician-CEO and an administrative team of newly hired professionals.

Data processing

Twice the Clinic completely changed the computer system and the personnel who operated it between 1985 and 1990.

Morale

Members of the Clinic acknowledged, and attrition and turnover figures confirmed, that morale of both physicians and employees was declining.

Financial

The Clinic's line of credit with its bank increased dramatically. For the first time, the Clinic established a capital reserve fund, but could not adequately fund it. Increased debt load made borrowing funds difficult, even for operations.

Recruitment

Recruitment became difficult, especially of the high earners. For the first time, the Clinic had to employ recruitment firms.

Decision making

Members of the Clinic frequently appealed the decisions made by the Board and committees. Lengthy delays in making and implementing decisions became common. The Clinic never did implement certain decisions. Over a five-year period, two separate committees studied cost accounting, but the Clinic's members would not accept any of their proposals.

Physical (objective) examination

Physicians' salaries and benefits decreased to approximately 43 percent of collected dollars.

Over a three-year period, the value of a share of stock in the Nalle Clinic diminished significantly.

Personnel turnover was averaging more than 20 percent per year.

Physicians who left were increasingly difficult to replace, and some positions lay vacant for long periods, resulting in significant problems with patient access.

HMO growth had stagnated at 35,000, and the Clinic stopped all marketing efforts because of inability to provide primary care to any more prepaid patients. In 1989 the fee-for-service equivalency on pre-paid activities fell to less than 75 percent.

Diagnostic work-up and initial treatment plan

Editor's note: The diagnostic work-up and initial treatment plan that Dr. Fernandez implemented are the subject of the case report which follows.

Overview of the case report

Irwin Rubin, PhD

WHEN A PHYSICIAN becomes the CEO of a health-care organisation, the entire organisation becomes that physician's patient, and the physician takes on a role we will refer to as *physician*-CEO. Other physicians provide essential leadership and managerial expertise formally in their roles as medical directors, chiefs of service, and department heads, and informally in their day-to-day practices. While these individuals may or may not have the well-being of the entire organisation in mind when they act, a physician-CEO must always have the well-being of the organisation in mind. The case that follows concerns such a physician, such an organisation, and the changes and growth that both are experiencing.

The five-year period of the chart entries we are about to examine is but a slice in time in the 70-year history of a proud organisation. We emphasise that this is *not* the story of a terminally-ill organisation trying to save itself. Rather, this is the story of a normal patient-organisation experiencing normal growing pains in a stressful environment. It is a story that thousands of health-care organisations are living at this very moment. In whatever form it is destined to grow, the institution will continue to be a living, breathing force searching for excellence in patient care.

The search for excellence is the foundation of the entire profession of medicine. Continuous improvement in quality care rests on publishing the results of intensive scrutiny of clinical cases. The classic method of case reports allows the sharing of experiences of successes and failures. This sharing helps the profession progress by allowing new generations to share the hard-earned knowledge of their predecessors without suffering through the pain of having to learn the same lessons in the same hard way. An array of hard new lessons present themselves daily as learning opportunities. Continuous improvement through experiential learning is critical, perhaps even more so when the patient is an entire organisation of providers.

In the chart we are about to review, one such physician, Dr. Raymond Fernandez, and one such organisation, the Nalle Clinic, courageously open their medical records for public scrutiny. (We will not include any information of a purely private or proprietary nature.) By allowing us a glimpse into the human nature of their encounters—as provider and patient—Dr. Fernandez and the Nalle Clinic are contributing to the changes and growth that an entire industry and its captains are experiencing. The opportunity to learn from their experience, without critical judgement, is a rare gift.

The case presentation has four parts. Following the outline of a typical patient work-up, Part One contains some of Dr. Fernandez's reflections, thoughts and feelings about the historical events leading up to his accepting the role of physician-CEO of the Nalle Clinic. This material is an edited version of a book chapter published in September 1988.[2]

Dr. Fernandez's and the Nalle Clinic's experiences reflect the massive developmental changes confronting the entire health-care industry. As each major chart entry will, Part One closes with a commentary. The intent of these commentaries is to stimulate you, the readers who share a common concern for improving the quality of patient care. The core of this first commentary is an article I published in 1987: "Organisations Have to Grow Up"[3] describes the stages of growth through which all health-care organisations, the Nalle Clinic being a single clinical example, must progress as they mature.

Having noted the patient's chief complaint and presenting symptoms, scanned its medical record, and reviewed elements of its history, we move to an examination of Dr. Fernandez's diagnostic work-up and initial treatment plan. Part Two offers us a glimpse of the patient's and provider's private medical records. Three memos, or chart entries, that Dr. Fernandez sent to his patient let us study leadership in action in organisational cultural change.

The anonymous questionnaire and open-group discussion that Dr. Fernandez refers to in the first memo reflect an X-ray diagnosis of his patient's initial state of health. These chart entries in Part Two will provide two things: first, a feel for the process of surveying a patient-organisation's human climate and, second, a glimpse of the issues and insights crucial to deciding on a treatment plan.

---

[2] Charles Raymond Fernandez, "Personal Managerial Evolution in a Multispecialty Clinic", *Roads to Medical Management*, ed. Wesley Curry, (Tampa: AAMD, 1988), pp. 74–77.
[3] "Organizations Have to Grow Up", *Physician Executive*, 13, no. 2, (March–April 1987), pp. 2–6.

Each of these chart entries freezes a moment in time: an encounter between a patient-organisation and its physician-CEO. These chart entries represent the first series of official interactions between patient and doctor. As such, they offer insights into the psychological contracting between the physician-CEO and his patient-organisation. This relationship mirrors the dynamics of early encounters between patients in pain and the providers they depend on for relief. Memos such as these give us insights into *what* physician-CEOs do and *how* they go about their practice.

Readers searching for formulas and therapies may find these chart entries and subsequent commentary incomplete. Just as each patient is unique, so is a patient-organisation. We will highlight general patterns and processes, not quick-fix solutions. Leadership in organisational cultural change requires the flexible and humane application of generic healing therapies to each organisation.

Part Three contains the edited transcripts of a tape Dr. Fernandez dictated and sent to Dr. Rubin on 5 December 1988. These personal chart entries give us a progress report of Dr. Fernandez's feelings some four years into his CEO relationship with his patient-organisation. The patient was experiencing predictable growing pains. The feelings Dr. Fernandez reports will enhance the logic and rationality of his first-person, historical introduction to Part One.

In addition to Dr. Rubin's commentaries, Part Three includes commentaries from five guest lecturers. Dr. Henry Berman, President and CEO of Group Health Northwest, is a seasoned veteran of the challenges of having an entire organisation as his patient. Dr. Kevin Sullivan, current Vice President of Medical Affairs of Port Huron Hospital, whose commentary follows Dr. Berman's, is a potential candidate for a position as physician-CEO. While Dr. Sullivan is responsible for a significant piece of his organisation, he does not, unlike Dr. Berman, occupy the seat where the buck stops. The commentaries of these two respected physicians, each at different stages of their own careers as leaders of organisational cultural change, add unique perspectives to the material Dr. Fernandez provides.

The final progress-report commentaries in Part Three speak to the shifting nature of the relationships between and among the central participants in the process of growing up. Keith Korenchuk, partner in the law firm of Parker, Poe, Adams & Bernstein, has served as the Nalle Clinic's attorney since 1982. His observations on the changing nature of legal issues—for example, stock ownership and restrictive covenants—balance the psychological contracting that has been our focus. Dr. John

7

Benedum is President of the Nalle Clinic Board and a long-standing friend and colleague of Dr. Fernandez's. Through his eyes we see the patient's view of the cultural change which occurred. Bruce Fritch is a consultant with extensive experience with organisations; his recent clients include the Nalle Clinic. His third-party insights concerning the shifting nature of the balance of power between physicians and patients have enormous implications for the entire health-care industry. Based on discussions with Mr. Fritch, Dr. Rubin added a commentary to Part Three: "Turbulent Passages of Change and the Dynamics of Power".

The chart entry in Part Four, the final section of this case, consists of newspaper articles and portions of taped conversations that occurred between 31 January and 5 March 1990, between Dr. Fernandez and his wife, Gail Fernandez. During this period the Nalle Clinic completed its current stage of development, and Dr. Fernandez's role as physician-CEO came to a close. As we shall be privileged to see in Part Four, Dr. Fernandez's feelings resonate more deeply and intensely as a natural, though often painful, part of the leadership of organisational cultural change.

While the facts and circumstances surrounding Dr. Fernandez's stepping down as physician-CEO in March 1990 have significance for him, his family, and the Nalle Clinic, we will not discuss them here. As a result, some will find the case incomplete. However, our objective is not to judge success—either of Dr. Fernandez as physician-CEO or of the Nalle Clinic as an organisation. Our objective is to identify, and learn from, some of the generic dynamics of leadership and organisational cultural change, particularly in the beginning and penultimate phases.

The final two commentaries in Part Four bring us full circle with our patient work-up. In "What's It All About, Alfie?" dated August 1990, Dr. Fernandez offers his prognosis. He addresses the questions, "What does all this change and its effect on me [as attending physician] and the organisation [as my patient] really mean?" and "What are the lessons here?" In "Human Parallels to Organisational Development" Dr. Rubin offers his prognosis of what this case suggests are the challenges faced by the health-care industry as it struggles in search of excellence in patient care.

We hope these commentaries and the entire case will encourage you to discuss your own experiences as physician and non-physician managers striving to bring the highest ideals of patient care to the practice of medicine.

Finally a word about the title we have chosen for the book. We call attention to *The Leadership Challenges* because its capital letters spell out TLC. While there is value to be drawn from DRGs (Diagnostically Related Groups), losing sight of the healing power of TLC could prove to be our most costly mistake. The most powerful ingredient of quality care cannot be commandeered or bought. Neither is it the sole responsibility of doctors and nurses. By caring for one another, every person in a provider organisation has the power to contribute to the creation of a healing culture.

We are all equal partners in meeting the leadership challenges in health care.

Part One

History

Chart entry

Historical events

Dr. Raymond Fernandez
September 1988

I KNOW OF NO school for physician-CEOs. To my knowledge, no educational curriculum alone can prepare one for this role. Thus, I offer
my description of my experiences as the first Medical Director and
Chief Executive Officer of the Nalle Clinic in the hope that it will help
bridge some gaps for others in health care who have accepted, or are
considering accepting, leadership roles.

The Nalle Clinic, a private, multi-speciality group in Charlotte,
North Carolina (population 500,000), has existed since 1921. I joined
the Clinic in 1975 as an internist and infectious-disease specialist. In less
than 15 years, it has grown more than in its previous 55 years, doubling
from 40 to nearly 80 physicians. This expansion and the many environmental changes facing medicine in general have greatly increased the
complexity of the organisation, changing a big small clinic into a small
big clinic. Currently the Clinic is making the transition from condominium orientation (physicians sharing facilities but running their own
practices) to a team approach to the delivery of medical care.

In 1978 the only administrative leadership role for a physician at the
Nalle Clinic was President of the Board of Directors. The physician
whom the Board elected President received neither compensation for
the position nor time to perform the duties of the office. At that time, a
task force studying whether the Clinic should have a medical director
rejected the position as a "waste of a physician's time".

However, critical duties such as recruiting physicians, planning for
the future, and disciplining physicians began to demand an inordinate
amount of the President's time. Finding people to serve on the Board
was also becoming difficult because of the commitment those duties
required. In 1981 the Board recognised that important decisions were

taking too long because the President's decision-making capacity was not adequate, and therefore decided to elect a physician to a management position as medical director. The medical director was to devote 50 percent of his time to administrative matters at a salary of 50 percent of the average Clinic physician's income. The idea was to financially motivate the medical director to improve the physicians' incomes.

The relationship of this new medical director to the non-physician administrative team was unclear. The Board did not spell out the position's power and authority, except to point out that the medical director would attend Board meetings in an advisory capacity but would not vote. The job description included such duties as planning, developing agendas for Board and committee meetings, communicating, and recruiting. Clearly, the medical director would need strong interpersonal, communication, problem-solving, and public-relations abilities.

When the Board elected me the Clinic's first Medical Director, one of my highest priorities was to obtain some type of training to give me the necessary background for my new position. Fortunately, one of the physicians in our group was active in the American Academy of Medical Directors (now the American College of Physician Executives) and pointed me towards its management courses. Programmes from the American Group Practice Association, the Medical Group Management Association, and the American Management Association also helped me to understand my new role. The Clinic provided an allowance to promote my education. However, as I believe everyone expected, most of my learning experience was on-the-job training and consisted of learning quickly from mistakes I made along the way.[4]

By 1983 I realised that 50 percent of my time was not adequate to perform all the duties of medical director and that I was also shortchanging my patients. The Board readily agreed to my suggestion that I devote 85 percent of my time to the medical director's duties. This change required that I give up all of my internal medicine practice, although I was able to keep my infectious disease consultant's role

---

[4] *Editor's note:* Dr. Fernandez's motivation and willingness to learn on the job can be seen, in part, from the changing nature of the titles prominent in his own library. Prior to 1985, Starr's *The Social Transformation of American Medicine*, Meisenheimer's *Quality Assurance*, and Roberts' *Rules of Order* were prime examples. A current review of his well-used library would uncover Peters, *et al.*'s *Thriving On Chaos* and *A Passion for Excellence*, Goldsmith's *Can Hospitals Survive?*, and Walton's *The Deming Management Method*.

relatively unchanged. Because I went off the call schedule,[5] members of my department who now had to cover for me faced increasing demands on their time. But at this point we all realised that my primary role had changed from being a clinician to being an administrator.

At a series of planning retreats in late 1984 and early 1985, the Board of Directors established a corporate structure for governing the Clinic. The Board staked out its authority to make decisions—even the tough, unpalatable ones. It designated for the first time the role of the chief executive officer, who would be in charge not only of the physician matters, now the duty of the medical director, but also of administrative matters. The CEO was to be the boss of the administrators as well as of the physicians. The Board invited me to accept that role.

---

[5] My call schedule hasn't changed since I took action to leave the Internal Medicine call schedule in 1983. I am on Infectious Disease call rotation—every 3–4 days; 1–3 consultations (each taking approximately 1 hour) in the hospital after regular work hours. Every fourth weekend I make hospital rounds and answer consults on Sat. and Sun. for 3 partners, which takes 4–8 hours per day on those days.

Commentary

Organisations have to grow up

Irwin Rubin, PhD

A HEALTH-CARE organisation is a living, breathing, human organism. There are hands-on providers and support personnel. Everyone, including management, is a semi-permanent member. This human healing organism—a hand-holding company—is the patients' contact when they visit this culture. Economically and humanely, the more temporary the patients' visit, the better.

As a consequence of their humanness, health-care organisations—like every social system—will reflect the entire range of human experience: they will go through good times and tough times. Right now the organised practice of medicine is dis-eased. Suspicion and mistrust characterise the provider-patient relationship. As a prerequisite to healing this relationship, to growing up, organisational cultures providing care will have to first heal themselves.[6]

Every institution is born from the seed of an idea. Like parents, its founding entrepreneurs put up with many sleepless nights and colicky outbursts. And, like a child, an organisation proceeds through predictable developmental phases. As someone's entrepreneurial baby struggles for an identity of its own, for the chance to grow beyond its biological and emotional roots, we can expect growing pains.[7] If the CEO is inhumanely replaced, the organisation may suffer a trauma as

---

[6] The initiation and management of this healing process will by led by physicians. The phenomenal growth of organisations such as the American College of Physician Executives confirms the fact that many physicians are preparing themselves to face the challenges of leadership in organisational cultural change.

[7] Decision-making dynamics are related to a team's age profile: therefore, individuals' mid-life crises can not be kept from the meeting room.

frightening as a flood of crushing chest pains. And not all organisations or industries will survive. Stronger corporate cells often take over, sometimes in a hostile way, organisations unable to learn from their experience and grow up. As the steel and automobile industries can attest, proud institutions do become extinct.

Organisations progress through a series of stages as they grow. How they handle themselves in each stage will determine how rapidly they progress to new stages, and whether they succeed to a new stage at all. Those organisations that adjust to growth most effectively become the standard setters that other organisations follow. We conceive, build, maintain, inhabit, and, when it is ill, heal, the human organism we call a health-care organisation.

There are three categories of issues that any organisation, like the Nalle Clinic, must address: mission, structure, and procedure. It is the responses to these issues and the processes by which the responses are made visible that define an organisation's stage of development. The degree of alignment determines effectiveness in any stage of development: does form (structure) fit with function (mission), and are both supported and reinforced by procedures?

Mission

Every organisation exists for a purpose. It has a mission, a direction, written or unwritten. As a result, a psychological contract operates between individual members and the organisation. This contract defines what individuals can expect to get and what they are expected to give. The contract is balanced when individuals' and the organisation's missions overlap.

Many mission statements are more rhetoric than reality. Consequently, the operational mission must often be inferred from behaviour. It is important to emphasise that the focus here is on how the organisation really operates, not on what appears in a formal statement. The Nalle Clinic's mission, as we shall see in Part Two, reflected a combination of desire and reality.

Structure

At its most basic level, the issue of structure involves questions of power. Who has what powers and upon what basis? As Dr. Fernandez has noted, "Important decisions were taking too long because the President's decision-making" power was no longer adequate. Structural changes were necessary. The formal organisational chart will be relevant, but it will not be the entire picture. An informal structure will develop: organisational bypasses will compensate for plugged arteries.

As was true with the mission, the operational structure most often will be inferred from observable patterns of behaviour. Particularly important will be patterns that develop around the management of differences, the organisation's response to conflict. Conflict situations represent arenas where individuals play out an organisation's legitimised power games. For example, there are status pecking orders in group-practice settings, with "real-doctor" surgeons at the top and general practitioners, family doctors, and "couldn't-hack-it-in-medical-school" psychiatrists lower down. Psychiatrists who care for the worried well and physicians who treat flu symptoms are more valued by their patients than by their organisational colleagues. These pecking orders will be reflected in the organisation's power structure.

Procedures

The underlying purpose behind any organisational procedure is to increase the probability that individuals' behaviours will support the mission. The procedures by which an organisation recruits, selects, and orients new members can, if aligned with the mission, attract people who already fit into the organisation.

Key among these procedures is the organisation's system of "consequence management". At issue here are the processes intended to address performance appraisals, rewards and punishments. There is also the issue of individual and organisational development via training, career development, and organisational succession. How does the organisation strive to guide the behaviour of members? The initial process of reviewing these structures and procedures at the Nalle Clinic began at a series of planning retreats in late 1984 and early 1985.

Before describing the three stages of organisational development, I want to emphasise the generic quality of these issues. Any two people who expect to develop and sustain a relationship must come to some agreement, often implicit, as to their mission in life. Their psychological contract speaks to what each can hope to get and will have to give to realise their common mission. The lack of agreement as to what constitutes "goodness", "quality", or "success"—mission-related issues—is the source of much conflict in intimate relationships.

Each couple—for instance, man and wife—will develop its own power structure. As men's and women's roles diverge from stereotypical roots, couples often find themselves at odds: she wants to explore her own career interests; he wants her to stay at home.

Mundane, day-to-day tasks essential to survival must be allocated and completed. Taking out the trash, scrubbing the bathrooms, and balancing the chequebook, while not as glamorous as performing rare surgical procedures, are pieces of the business of living. Each couple needs to resolve its conflicts ("All right. This Thanksgiving we'll go to your mother's. But we'll spend Christmas with my dad"), to make unpopular decisions, and to complete unappealing chores.

As with individuals and organisations, couples move through various stages of development. The exhilarating "no-one-else-exists-in-the-world-but-us", care-free glow of the honeymoon period passes into the need to grow up, to get down to the business of taking life one day at a time.

Now let's look at the three stages of organisational development.

Stage 1: the fraternity model

Many health-care organisations, group practices in particular, are remarkably similar to college fraternities. Individual freedom of expression is the central driving force. Each person is highly committed to selfish special interests (e.g., area of study). The primary reason for being together is not task interdependence.

Individual member commitment is time-bounded (e.g., four years at college). Dues will be paid "as long as I get what I want". This fraternity orientation feeds, and is consistent with, a mind set of low tolerance for delayed gratification. In psychological terms, the fraternity-model organisation stimulates and feeds what Maslow called lower-order human needs. The primary focus is on self-satisfaction and personal security. Goodies—such as money, time off, and trips to professional-development meetings in Hawaii and Bermuda—like food on the frat dinner table, are grabbed by those with the longest reach and quickest hands.

Mission issues

Regardless of what the written version may be, the operational mission of a fraternity-model health-care organisation is the satisfaction of individual member's and/or owner's needs. The organisation exists to satisfy the immediate needs of its most powerful members. Individuals give up some security and opportunities for synergy. In return, they get relatively high degrees of individual freedom and minimal organisational control. In its most extreme form, the mind set is one of "renting space from the administrative entity" with all the consequent grumbling about overhead.

Structure issues

A health-care organisation at this stage of development is replete with a host of we-they dynamics: physicians mistrust administrators; surgeons look askance at family practitioners; nurses align themselves with their doctors; and founding seniors tolerate "young Turks".

Formal role constraints are minimal. Indeed, the formal organisation charts are quite flat, particularly on the medical side. Physician managers are often figureheads, with more administrative than managerial responsibilities. They are more reactive than proactive.

Where stock ownership is a factor, a variety of blackball dynamics show up. The board regularly finds hours of hard work overturned by a single stockholder. Professional, non-physician administrators defend themselves against stockholders who bemoan how "their" hard-earned dollars are being spent. It should come as no surprise that conflict avoidance pervades the organisation.

Procedures

A high degree of randomness and/or lack of selectiveness characterises the new membership process. Often, a new member is the friend of a current member, and trial memberships of varying lengths are typical before someone achieves what amounts to tenure.

Many a fraternity-model health-care organisation is surprised at how many behaviour problems show up shortly after a new member becomes a stockholder. Such a turn of events should surprise no one; the absence of such examples would be a surprise. Individuals rushing a fraternity are on their good behaviour during hazing. Behaviour problems are unlikely to surface until after the ritualistic induction into the brotherhood.

Systems of formalised performance appraisal, if they exist at all on the medical side, focus exclusively on broad standards of patient care. Similarly, in a fraternity individuals enjoy wide behavioural boundaries. All manner of acting out is tolerated as long as it does not threaten the basic sanctity of the brotherhood. That is, it is all right to get drunk and rowdy at parties as long as neighbours don't call the police. Constraints on personal behaviour in fraternity-like organisations are virtually non-existent, as is any formalised reward-and-punishment system, short of termination.

Given the fraternity orientation, short-range income concerns consume the organisation. Members spend hours designing and reworking salary formulas. Even more energy is spent in maintaining the system by those who benefit, in reaction to those who feel short-changed. Almost everyone gets a chance to be in each group more than once.

Organisationally supported development is infrequent or non-existent. Time for professional development might be granted if the production formula takes this time into account. Organisational development for physicians taking on managerial responsibilities receives token financial support and even less emotional support.

Stage II: the basic business organisation

If a Stage-I organisation is characterised by a childlike orientation, Stage II is akin to a young-adult orientation. The underlying theme is "Let's get serious, let's get down to business". Degrees of task interdependence are accepted. Delayed gratification becomes a tolerated reality.

The organisation's long-term investment strategies reflect this expectation. There will be reserves set aside for new facilities to ensure the continuing growth and replacement of the physical plant, although individuals who are holding on to the Stage-I fraternity mentality will resist having to sign their names to long-term mortgage notes for new facilities. There will be new retirement programmes allowing individuals to defer income to later stages of their personal life cycles. Organisational contributions and vesting conditions are often hotly contested issues.

The design and implementation of these longer-term investment strategies require careful planning. Like the Stage-II organisational culture in which they are embedded, they are intended, in psychological terms, to stimulate and feed Maslow's middle-level needs for belonging and self-esteem. But to those who are more comfortable in a fraternity-type organisation, golden parachutes can become golden handcuffs. Individuals who feel imprisoned by long-term promises can become embittered, poisoning their own and others' senses of belonging and self-esteem.

Mission issues

The operational mission of a Stage-II organisation is survival, adaptation, and growth in its external market environment, which is hostile and competitive. The organisation's formal mission, if it exists, focuses on achieving short-term results, such as improving the fee-for-service vs. HMO-income ratio by x% and decreasing billing times.

The operating psychological contract shifts accordingly. People give up some individuality and accept more organisational control. In return, they get the security offered by an organisation and the attendant economies of scale.

The mind set is "You work for, and are protected by, the organisation". This has a much higher level of psychological commitment than simply "renting space". Consequently, the structure is different.

Structure issues

While power differences still exist, they are somewhat less imbalanced, the degree varying according to the strength and maturity of the organisation. The basic hierarchical model remains the underlying structure in Stage II. Loose, informal boundaries of Stage I are replaced by very careful, formalised role descriptions. The medical side of the organisation, while still relatively flat, now has physician managers with varying degrees of positional power and personal training.

Blackball dynamics have given way, often grudgingly, to more democratic actions. In the strongest Stage-II organisations, decision-making protocols ("who is to be involved?" "how?" in "what decisions?"), have become formalised procedures that minimise the day-to-day squabbles of the fraternity model.

Resolving conflicts is essential, so avoidance is no longer the dominant orientation. Minimising emotional heat remains the primary unspoken objective. Compromising (resulting in both parties being half-satisfied) or forcing (by those with the positional power to do so) become the dominant modes of conflict management.

Procedures

The importance of the organisation, its need to outlive any single member, manifests itself in more rationalised systems of recruitment, selection, and orientation. The organisation hires professional search firms. Personnel applying for jobs may have to take psychological tests. *What* you know and *what* you've done become more important than *who* you know.

In the most mature Stage-II organisations, formalised performance appraisal systems begin to appear *throughout* the organisation. Only a small number of Stage-II health-care organisations step up to the need to define and assess the interpersonal behaviours of their physician members. Indeed, the way in which Stage-II organisations handle this procedural issue will be a major factor in their movement into, and level of growth within, this stage of organisational development.

Income will remain an important concern. Mature Stage-II organisations develop mechanisms to depersonalise and rationalise the process. This means a formula must be agreed upon. It will tie individual salaries to measurable behaviours deemed relevant (at least in theory), to the achievement of the agreed-upon mission. While the result may be a mechanistic, impersonal formula, the process of designing the formal reward system will be emotionally charged and personal. At this point the day-to-day meaning of the mission's words on paper come to life.

How much is it worth to the organisation, to that elusive commodity called quality care, to see one more patient/hour versus scheduling slack time so patients can talk? How much is it worth to inconvenience the physicians by having full evening and weekend office coverage versus meeting patients' needs for access? "My short-term income as a practitioner may drop if we hire a new physician now. On the other hand, patients may not need to wait months for an appointment".

In designing their compensation formula, Stage-II organisations are putting their money where their mouth is. Little wonder that enormous numbers of hours go into the design of the compensation system. In the most mature form of the Stage-II organisations, once hashed out, the issue is (with the exception of minor adjustments), put to bed. In contrast, members of the immature Stage-II organisations, like fraternity members, return to this formula and try to squeeze out more for themselves every chance they get.

Whereas fraternity-model organisations spend little on individual and/or organisational development, Stage-II organisations do invest in such programmes. Medical management, for example, becomes valued enough to develop and pay for, even though the attitude about it is still defensive. But when the external environment gets tough, a Stage-II organisation will typically seek to cut its development budget.

Moving from Stage I to Stage II

It is important that we examine what conditions are necessary for an organisation to consciously move from Stage I to Stage II. Strengthening these conditions will enhance an organisation's growth as a Stage-II entity.

The mechanics of the shift

The organisational mechanisms needed to move from Stage I to Stage II are not the least bit mysterious. A mission statement focusing on clear, concise, quantitative goals is the starting point. Then monitoring systems, planning functions, and formal statements of authority and responsibility can be designed to attain mission goals.

At the procedural level, the key issue revolves around the performance-appraisal system. It makes absolutely no sense to develop an organisational mission if performance appraisal is to be left as an abstraction. People need to know what they are expected to do. These behaviours need to be agreed upon, defined, measured, and fed back.

While help may be gained from outside the organisation, the final answer—what equals "good behaviour"—must come from within. The unwillingness and inability of a health-care organisation to step up to this issue, particularly as it relates to physicians (who may also be owners), keeps many at Stage I or ensures that growth within Stage II is stymied. (The same is true of individuals. As we struggle to grow up, we increasingly take responsibility for our own behaviour.)

In the extreme, this is the procedure that decides ultimately whether a single individual is bigger than the organisation. There will be instances in which a "bottom-line" decision must be made on a very high-income producer who refuses, or is unable, to behave in harmony with the mission.

Hostage high-jacking dramas are played out with frightening regularity. Because of speciality and extraordinary technical competence, for example, a surgeon may generate millions of dollars in gross revenues, not to mention a hefty personal income. On many occasions this same physician regularly exhibits behaviours that fall, if not outside the letter of the mission, certainly outside its spirit. For example, a physician schedules a golf game and tells a nurse to cancel a patient's appointment. If the nurse, the front-line provider of TLC, questions these priorities, the nurse may be verbally abused by the prima-donna high earner.

A 1990 court ruling in San Antonio, Texas,[8] drove home the financial, not to mention professional, implications of an organisation's

---

[8] James E. Schutte, "An Impaired Doctor Cost His Colleagues $5 Million", *Medical Economics*, (4 June 1990), pp. 45–50.

contributing to hostage dynamics. A patient's malpractice suit involved a host of other physicians as accomplices because it could be proven that they knew her physician—their colleague—was impaired and not delivering quality care. The $5 million settlement ought to send a much-needed message as to the real bottom-line decisions confronting the profession.

The underlying attitude behind the shift

The major attitude shift in moving from Stage I to Stage II has to do with the perceived value of the organisation and management. For a successful transition to Stage II, the managerial function must be believed to *add value* as opposed to being seen as an overhead expense. The seriousness of this belief system will be seen, or not, in the way the organisation selects, trains, rewards, and otherwise supports its managers, whose responsibility, in turn, is to ensure that all of the organisation's assets—human and otherwise—are effectively and efficiently aligned with the mission.

As a consequence, some individuals will not want, or be able, to stay. Many will have consciously joined a fraternity model and only be happy in that form of organisation. As humanely as possible, they need to be helped to find an environment that better fits their needs.

How long should such a transition from Stage I to Stage II take? Absolute numbers are impossible to provide. A minimum of 3–5 years would not be surprising. The resources involved to cover *expected* and *necessary* training to support the development of new behavioural patterns, not needed in Stage I, will be extensive. The amount will be a function of how long the organisation has been in Stage I and how strong a Stage-II organisation it hopes to become.

Stage III: an organisation in search of excellence

A Stage-III organisation has a mature adult orientation. The organisation and its members have a holistic orientation. Everyone feels empowered by task interdependence. The resulting need for high-level teamwork is not considered a necessary evil.

Consequently, individual members thrive on challenge, trust, change, and innovation. In psychological terms, a Stage-III organisation meets all of Maslow's lower-order/middle-order needs and stimulates and feeds higher-order needs for self-actualisation. The required shift in mind set is dramatic, as one would expect given the potential benefits to be realised. It is a quantum leap, *not* a mere extrapolation.

Mission

The mission of a Stage-III organisation steps beyond merely reacting to a basically hostile external environment. This organisation strives to be a standard setter that Stage-II organisations follow. The organisation's formal mission, which will certainly appear on paper, focuses on the achievement of long-term, hard-to-measure, *qualitative* values. One such organisation, on the verge of beginning a continuing search for excellence, unashamedly and sincerely has the words *love, joy*, and *nurturance* in its mission statement.

The operating psychological contract for a Stage-III organisation is unique and expensive. The organisation provides security from arbitrary layoffs, but not from dismissal for continued unacceptable performance. It also provides regular opportunities for challenge, autonomy, and synergy. In return, individual members are expected to give up a piece of their *souls*—to invest their *selves* in the business.

The mind set of Stage-III people is "I am the organisation". When numerous individuals feel as if the organisation is *their* business, they attend carefully to their investment. It is rational selfish behaviour with win-win consequences.

Structure

In such a psychological climate, we note a significant change in the power dynamics. No longer is rigid hierarchy necessary or relevant. Personal power is more important than formal position. The mission, not turf battles, is paramount. Organisations in search of excellence are both "tight and loose". As Peters and Waterman have so carefully documented,[9] they are fluid.

Given the inadvisability of always relying on "the boss" to resolve conflicts, individuals are required to develop a win-win orientation. They confront their differences within the powerful common ground afforded by the organisation's mission. Pooling and sharing all income, increasingly common among forward-thinking groups and departments, is a far cry from the me-first grabbing that characterises a Stage-I mentality.

---

[9] Thomas J. Peters and Robert H. Waterman, Jr., *In Search of Excellence*, (New York: Harper & Row, 1982), pp. 318–325.

What keeps people on track? The rigid hierarchical structure of a Stage-II organisation tells people that they need supervision. But the operating structure of an organisation in search of excellence relegates control to a trust-based SUPER VISION.

Procedures

We talk easily of "the system" as if it were a God-given entity rather than a creation of our minds. Stage-III organisations know better. They know that organisations in search of excellence are made of *individuals* who are in search of excellence, and that self-actualising individuals will create self-actualising organisations. Organisations in search of excellence put enormous energy into recruitment, selection, and orientation. They try to help people to self-select. For example, one very large high-tech organisation in search of excellence requires, by its mission, people who see themselves as innovative entrepreneurs. The opening line in its new-hire advertisements announces that "Digital Equipment (DEC) is looking for *individual contributors* in the area of ... ". Many candidates react with the thought, "Individual contributor? All I want is a job!" DEC breathes a sigh of relief as one unlikely fit self-selects out!

With respect to orientation, Disney World provides other organisations with food for thought. A summer employee who works for only 10 weeks gets five days (10%!) of orientation training. At the end of that period, if the mission requirement of treating all customers as "guests in someone's home" has not been internalised, the candidate is released.

Organisations in search of excellence recognise that everyone has "customers". A boss has subordinates as customers. Numerous formal and informal mechanisms exist to ensure that everyone gets customer feedback. Rather than fear this continuous feedback, members seek and thrive on it. These organisations recognise that as individuals grow and develop, the organisation will, too. IBM, a clear standard setter in this regard, invested over $1 billion in 1985 to support the development of its 300,000 employees. The 40,000 people who wear the mantle "manager" must, by IBM's requirements, take two weeks of management development each year. When the external environment gets tough, Stage-III organisations typically seek to *increase* their development budgets.

I would like to illustrate how one health-care organisation treats its members and its patients "as guests in someone's home".

Because she is the first person visitors meet when they enter the lobby, the official greeter is one of the most important and respected persons at St. Marguerite Hospital, Chiba, Japan. So vital is her role to the success of the business that her position requires a minimum of ten years of experience as a nurse. The woman who greeted me on 2 March 1988, was in her late 50s and had been a nurse for more than 30 years. As I soon learned, this attention to the human component of quality care permeates St. Marguerite.

My official host was 60-year-old Dr. Seiichi Satoh. The previous day, he had participated in a seminar I conducted on health-care management in the US. He said that he would be honoured if I would visit his hospital. He was eager to learn all he could to help his hospital.

St. Marguerite's mission is simple and straightforward. To paraphrase Dr. Satoh, "Although people do not wish enthusiastically to go to the hospital, if they must go, we intend to have them choose happily to consult St. Marguerite". The hospital's brochure promises total medical service, high tech and human touch, hand in hand in pursuit of St. Marguerite's goal: to provide quality care and quality life in a resort atmosphere on a foundation of human kindness. The words embossed on the plaque outside the front door introduce the promise:

To heal sometimes
To support often
To comfort always

The hospital cares well for its healthy elderly. An elevator-like stretcher lowers the incapacitated into the warm-water bath so culturally critical to the cleansing of their bodies and souls. Along with an Olympic-size pool (the kindest exercise), and flamenco dance (great for flexibility), St. Marguerite provides English lessons because many patients wish to visit the US before they die. The hospital planned to break ground soon for a hospice.

In the dormitory-style hospital rooms, ample breathing space between the six beds is the norm. For those who can afford them, private rooms are available. The hospital also provides space for family members to sleep, with either futon or Western-style beds.

The secret of St. Marguerite Hospital is no secret at all. It's the same message that has been available to us from the Japanese for years. Our own excellence research has uncovered similar truths, which we all reacted to as being common sense. Still, we have yet to explain why such common sense is so uncommon a reality. The key to excellence begins and ends with how the staff treat one another.

I asked Dr. Satoh how St. Marguerite's management had inculcated human kindness into the organisation. (A professional staff of 8 full-time and 13 part-time physicians and 70 nurses forms the core of the total staff of 160 at St. Marguerite. Five people hold full-time managerial positions.) Careful selection of staff was the start, he said, but just the start. For the six months prior to the opening of the new, expanded services in October of 1987, which took the hospital from 200 beds to 315, the two most senior managers, including the equivalent of a Western medical director, spent the better part of every day walking around St. Marguerite, talking to the staff about the importance of kindness. We call this ritual MBWA, management by walking around, and it's a ritual they perform with daily regularity and undocumented impact.

To his answer I can only add my own observations. The respect Dr. Satoh showed all the other staff was, in one sense, purely Japanese. Arriving on a floor, we first stopped at the nurse's station. Without my daughter and son-in-law along to interpret, I would have followed right on Dr. Satoh's heels, not understanding his request that I wait a moment. Before taking us onto a floor, several of which were still empty, Dr. Satoh needed to announce and explain our presence and to request permission to enter. Dr. Satoh, a most senior physician, requested permission to enter! A warmly smiling nurse or nurse's aide scurried along beside us in case we required any assistance. We could examine equipment, even if it was not in use, only after Dr. Satoh had briefed the attending physician.

I didn't understand any of the conversations between Dr. Satoh and the people with whom he spoke during my tour. Despite the best efforts of my daughter and son-in-law to translate, we missed many of the words. But respect and kindness transcend the boundaries of language and culture. In a way that is consistent with their culture, the people of St. Marguerite Hospital afforded me and one another immeasurable respect and kindness. They have much to teach us about how to turn common sense into common human service.

The quantum leap

If it does make great sense to treat human resources in a Stage-III manner, we must ask, "Why do few organisations venture out of the security of Stage II to embark on a search for excellence?" We hypothesised that the implicit mission of a Stage-II organisation is survival, adaptation, and growth within a basically competitive, hostile, external market environment. So the resultant formal mission statement emphasises short-run quantitative goals. As a result, an organisation develops an emphasis on *not losing*.

An organisation in search of excellence has made a conscious choice to move to a higher plane than its Stage-II colleagues. Given the need to engage people's souls, a mission that reaches deeply into untapped human potential must be formulated. This means focusing on deeply held values. The collective mind set is upon winning something that really matters to people's souls, a dramatically different attitude from "not losing". Within a mind set of winning, there are no mistakes. There are only valuable learning experiences.

The mentality of *doing whatever needs to be done* is crucial to the search for excellence. An organisation will have to design its own new structures and procedures continuously. Successes will fuel the motivation to move to the next plateau of achievement. As customers and members get used to excellence, their standards go up. To meet rising expectations, managers will have to invent new solutions. Yesterday's success will be the training ground for tomorrow's challenge, not necessarily the answer to tomorrow's challenge.

This mentality is infinitely easier to write about than to implement. It flies in the face of much managerial folklore and practice. "If it ain't broke, don't mess with it" is one such attitude, and it may minimise losing. At the same time, it ensures minimal innovation. Managerial practice and education are long on problem solving—hunting down and rooting out causes of mistakes—and frightfully short on success management—identifying and spreading out causes of successes. Organisations in search of excellence know better, which is why they function better.

The toughness that develops while succeeding in Stage II provides the strength to venture into Stage III. But success is not guaranteed. Success during Stage II depends primarily upon the depth and quality of managerial talent available. Managers are responsible for "doing things right". They focus on keeping the organisation on course. Management by objectives, MBO, captures the essence of this responsibility.

Entering and succeeding in Stage III requires acts of leadership. Whereas a Stage-II manager focuses on "doing things right", a Stage-III leader focuses on the question, "What is the right thing to do?" Rather than being a play on words, these phrases represent two dramatically different mind sets. The natural tension between them is the hallmark of an organisation in search of excellence. It is the constant tension between "Who are we? How are we doing?" and "Who could we be? How could we get there?"

Application to the Nalle Clinic

Let's turn from a description of the three stages to our study of the Nalle Clinic. The Nalle Clinic, as the patient-organisation and Dr. Fernandez, as its physician-CEO providing the needed guidance, met formally when the patient was in its mid-sixties. In chronological terms, the patient-organisation was not young. In developmental terms, it mirrored a "Stage-I fraternity model". (The Clinic's term was "medical condominium".) The Clinic wanted to change its mind set to that of a "Stage-II basic business organisation". To accomplish this, members of the Clinic would have to change their commitment from "I rent space from an administrative entity" to "We work for the organisation, and it protects us".

In developmental terms, the patient's chief complaint, presenting illness, and past history all suggest a gangling adolescent struggling to grow beyond its childhood. The teenager learns that not only does he live in a house with his family, he must act as a team member with his siblings and parents. In the same way, the physicians needed to change their orientations from, as Dr. Fernandez put it, "physicians sharing facilities, but running their own practices" to "a team approach to medical care". The search for excellence forces us to continuously decide *what* we want to be when we grow up and *how* to get there.

Many balk at the notion of excellence: "It is an ideal! It can never be achieved!" Their dilemma is one of perspective: they see "it"—excellence—as a specific, finite place where we arrive; they don't see it as the quality of the journey we are all on. In that sense we never "grow up"; instead we are continuously in the process of growing up. The dissatisfaction and emptiness many "successful" senior executives feel at the peak of their careers reflects the processes used (or abused) in getting to the top. For example, many executives missed their child's second birthday party or their first little-league home run. In short, they traded time with their families for time with their careers. And then they feel lonely at the top. The nature and quality of our process of growing up will determine the success we experience along the way.

Like that of a rebellious adolescent, the patient-organisation's initial posture towards management and leadership, towards care from its providers, was a 50-50 split. The appointment of a medical director who was "to devote 50 percent of his time to administrative matters at a salary of 50 percent of the average Clinic physician's income" replaced zero compensation for the "waste of a physician's time".

Human nature seeks to have its cake and eat it, too. Humans expect to be cured without taking responsibility for their own wellness. Placing unclear lines of authority and power in the hands of a person whose medical training has not given him the strong interpersonal communication, problem-solving, and public relations abilities necessary for success has the earmarks of an impossible mission. The fact that physicians dominate the patient-organisation complicates this mission in several ways.

Patients tend to give up too much power to their doctors, treating them like gods. Physicians, on the other hand, have great difficulty relinquishing control under any circumstances, particularly when they are in the patient role. Organisational cultural change will shift the balance of power away from individual physicians. In a similar vein, many of the members of the Nalle Clinic grew up professionally during the golden age of physician power, 1955 to 1985. The sense of entitlement they developed is shifting uneasily as the entire medical profession matures. Doctor-driven organisations will regularly present their physician-CEOs with the challenges of managing non-compliant patients.

Leadership in organisational cultural change requires intuitive and formal skills. Fortunately, educational support was available for Dr. Fernandez. Still, he expected—as he believed others did—that most of his learning would be experiential, "from mistakes [he] made along the way".

By 1983 the 50-50 bargain was more than Dr. Fernandez could tolerate. His integrity was at stake: "I realised that 50 percent of my time was not adequate to perform all the duties of medical director and that I was also short-changing my patients". A major emotional and cognitive shift was necessary: he had to devote all his time to one patient, an entire organisation of care-providers.

In late 1984 the Board invited Dr. Fernandez to quarterback the Nalle Clinic's life-support team during a period of transition. The Board invited him to accept the role of CEO, "the boss of the administrators as well as the physicians". It was a role for which no job description existed; it was a role without a school, other than experience, to learn from.

What Dr. Fernandez did and said—his style of communication—and how he provided life support, technically and humanely, were the tools of his practice as he struggled to care for his patient-organisation. As a physician-CEO, he had to learn to act honourably, with persistence.

In Part Two, we examine through three early chart entries, concrete manifestations of this reality.

Part Two

Diagnostic work-up and initial treatment plan

Chart entry

Memorandum

To: All staff
From: CEO
Date: 13 December 1984
Subject: Nalle Clinic Organisation Workshop

TWO WEEKENDS ago, the Board of Directors met in a retreat and made decisions that will have significant implications for all members of the Nalle Clinic family. The Board is redefining the mission of the Clinic.

A seminar that Dr. Irv Rubin conducted this past weekend helped members of the Clinic analyse, not only our strengths, but also our weaknesses. Not only physicians and administrators but several people representing other employees of the Clinic attended this seminar. The seminar was beneficial because it made clear that administration is not always best qualified to make decisions on any given matter. In fact, those closest to the problem frequently have the best solution. We have proven this theory over and over in the many task forces that have worked on specific problems in recent months. Their efforts proved that input from a broad range of people leads to the best decisions.

Several weeks ago, many of us filled out questionnaires on our attitudes about the Clinic. The data from these questionnaires reveal a profile of where we stand and what some of our problems are.

- Morale of physicians and employees is nowhere near ideal.
- Considerable confusion exists about our mission and goals.
- Considerable confusion also exists about the chain of command. Commonly, a person trying to get a solution to a problem will go to several other people in different positions, leading to wasted energy as well as frustration.
- A tremendous lack of decisiveness results from no one's being clear

on who has authority to do what. This lack of decisiveness runs through the entire organisation, from the Board of Directors down to the supervisors.

- Most employees aspire to quite high standards, and in some cases they expect more of themselves than those in leadership do. Occasionally, people make decisions more on the basis of what is good for the physicians than what is good for the employees or even for the patients.
- Commonly, members of one group or department don't listen to other groups.
- Too little co-operation exists between departments. When one division needs temporary help, too few individuals from other divisions volunteer. Protecting one's own division at the expense of another's erodes trust.
- Even within the same department, one person is unwilling to assist another.
- We lack a well-developed reward system. Too often, someone who does a job well doesn't receive even a pat on the back.
- Even more often, we do not invoke sanctions for someone who is doing a mediocre job, just squeaking by.
- We have no formal training programme to develop leadership skills. We tend to promote people to supervisory positions without training them and allowing them to develop appropriate skills to handle their new roles.
- We cannot easily or suddenly change the culture we have evolved. We will have to strengthen many links in the chain of command.
- We are hiring a professional personnel manager who will assist not only in recruiting the highest-calibre personnel but also in training supervisors and in team building.
- We will recruit a new Clinic manager ... to help identify and handle many of the Clinic's everyday problems.
- The Board of Directors is restructuring the entire administrative team and has appointed Dr. Fernandez to quarterback the team as Chief Executive Officer.
- The Board will have a four-day retreat in late January to plan new projects the Clinic will be taking on.
- The Board will also authorise new committees to handle the various tasks necessary to provide strong leadership in the Clinic.
- The Board will ask employees to participate in more task forces to help deal with specific problems.
- Our supervisors will take on new and greater responsibilities.

In short, we will ask all in the organisation to elevate their standards of performance. Together, we can push one another to move the Clinic forward.

None of these changes will be easy, simple, or quick. Some of them will be hard for some people to accept. Many of us have grown comfortable in our current roles and would rather not strive for higher levels of performance. However, with the commitment that so many physicians and employees have already shown, we can't fail. Too many people have already invested significant energy in these changes. We have a lot of smart, dedicated people committed to this project. They have been willing to look at our weaknesses and to make plans to correct them. We have allowed several outside consultants to come in and analyse us. Our leadership is strongly committed to this project and has resolved not to let it fizzle, even when the going gets tough. A new, shared sense of our commitment to be the pre-eminent health-care organisation in this region will be our motivation. This shared sense of mission will convert us from a loosely associated group of individual practitioners into a real organisation, in the grandest sense of the word.

Editor's note: Sixteen of the physicians and non-physicians involved in the planning retreat wrote evaluations. Their comments were uniformly positive and optimistic.

Chart entry

Memorandum

To: All staff
From: CEO
Date: 27 January 1985
Subject: Report of long-range planning retreat

THE EXECUTIVE TEAM participated in a long-range planning retreat 24–27 January at Black Mountain. Mr. Bruce Fritch co-ordinated this planning work. In the past, some of the Clinic's policies and decisions have been reactions to problems. In recent months, sentiment has been building for active decision-making that would anticipate, even avoid, problems. Only when we understand the big picture of where the Clinic wants to go can we align individual decisions with our goals.

The attached "Mission Statement of the Nalle Clinic" sets forth the Clinic's objectives. Please notice the commitment to providing high-quality patient-care through a team approach. By uniting us in this common effort, our mission will provide us many advantages, not the least of which is a more rewarding work environment. To achieve this goal, all of us must have the same vision of what we want our new Clinic to be.

We thoroughly analysed both the strengths and the weaknesses of the various areas of the Clinic and concluded that nineteen separate areas need specific plans for improvement. These include financial management, growth, administrative systems, marketing, community participation, human-resource development, and performance measurement and assessment.

In the next several days, we will appoint members to each of the twelve priority task forces created. We will appoint and train team leaders and educate teams about their specific roles as well as how they fit into the larger perspective of the Clinic's planning and decision making.

They will receive support in the form of the personnel or finances necessary to accomplish their specific tasks. They will report their activities and recommendations to the Board of Directors and, ultimately, to all personnel of the Clinic. The Board will also provide co-ordinators to increase the efficiency of the work of these groups. We will establish specific schedules for completing these actions. The Board will also continue its long-range planning.

This approach is a distinct departure from past methods of making decisions about problems. The quality of our decisions should improve dramatically. The result of this effort should be a more integrated clinic where all personnel will more clearly comprehend their roles in the organisation and will, therefore, be able to make more significant contributions. Every role is critical to the success of the organisation.

Past efforts like this in the Nalle Clinic and in other organisations have proven that these endeavours are worth the effort. The Board hopes that its commitment to improving the Clinic will flow down to all levels of the Clinic. If we can all pick up their enthusiasm, the Nalle Clinic's stature will skyrocket. Working in a clinic whose goal is to become the pre-eminent health-care facility in this region of the country will actually be fun. Our pride should be sufficient reward for the time, money, and energy the Clinic is committing.

The Board has set up a framework for success. In a short time, specific fruits of this labour should become apparent. When we ask you to make your contribution, please remember that your participation is essential to the overall success of our mission.

Chart entry

Mission statement of the Nalle Clinic

THE NALLE CLINIC will provide to our patients comprehensive health care of the highest quality. In this cause, our organisational structure will give maximum support to our personnel.

We pledge that we will use our energies and talents to provide medical care that is compassionate and personal, cost efficient and convenient. In addition, we will offer innovative services and health-care programmes.

We will recruit only the finest, most-qualified staff; conduct clinical research; commit to broad-based involvement in quality assessment; and encourage an effective education programme for physicians, staff, patients, and community.

We dedicate ourselves to visionary leadership in medical and business practices, being ever mindful of our commitment to the unique individuals who constitute the Nalle Clinic. We will nurture their growth and pride in the organisation.

We will preserve and enhance the integrity of the Clinic and will strive to be a source of comfort and support to the community.

By direction of the Board of Directors
27 January 1985

Chart entry

Letter

To Irv Rubin
From Raymond Fernandez, MD
Date 1 February 1985

Dear Irv

I have included a copy of our Mission Statement as well as a report to all of our personnel about the success of the long-range planning effort. Bruce Fritch's leadership of the Board in this effort was masterful. I was also tickled with the tremendous energy and commitment the Board exhibited in approaching this task.

I sense an understanding that "things are happening" permeating our organisation, and a growing commitment to those things. It's not all easy, and some people are standing back in disbelief and with a challenging attitude. With time and patience, I think we will win their support.

Wouldn't it be wonderful if everyone in our organisation could pick up some of the understanding that I obtained from your course? ... I hope that Bruce will be able to do the same type of job here at the Clinic. I will certainly support him in that effort, and I encourage you to help walk him through the steps necessary to get to that position.

Commentary

Organisational culture change: a self-help programme

Irwin Rubin, PhD

W HAT IS ESSENTIAL to quality patient care? Active commitment to, and full participation in, healing. As physician-CEO, Dr. Fernandez is dedicated to the Nalle Clinic. Though the patient has lots of different ideas and concerns, he keeps lines of communication open. He provides forums, structures, information, and communication skills. In so doing, he adapts and replicates a process used regularly by physicians in dealing with patients: the Weed process.

Quality care requires freedom of choice, commitment, full participation, and valid data, both subjective and objective. As the attending physician for the Nalle Clinic, Dr. Fernandez begins by interviewing his patient (13 December 1984, memo). Together they make a thorough diagnosis of the Clinic's current state of health. Anonymous questionnaires are supplemented by publicly aired beliefs, pains, and anxieties. Through Dr. Fernandez's leadership, the patient begins taking personal responsibility for its own wellness. Influential parts of the patient are beginning to take action to heal themselves.

Individual patients take responsibility for their own wellness by having periodic medical check-ups, including X-ray diagnoses of the functioning and health of vital internal organs. Similarly, health-care organisations intent on growing up, regardless of their stage of development, will begin by diagnosing their climate. For Stage-III organisations, such X-ray diagnoses are matters of regularly scheduled organisational health maintenance.

An organisation's climate, the working atmosphere that prevails within the organisation, has proven to be a strong indicator of the organisation's health and performance. All of us respond to our environment.

If we are uncomfortable in particular surroundings, we focus on that discomfort and use our energy to deal with the circumstances creating it. In a win-win organisational climate, individuals co-operate in striving for their common goal: excellence in patient-centred quality care.

The anonymous questionnaire and open-group discussion that Dr. Fernandez refers to in his 13 December 1984 memo reflect such an X-ray diagnosis of his patient's health. This diagnosis contains few surprises.[10] The process used, however, brings unrecorded hallway and coffee-room conversations into the open and increases people's commitment to take action. What follows will give you a taste of the process and a glimpse of the issues and insights such a diagnosis can provide. We'll highlight general qualitative patterns and themes, not detailed specific quantitative results.

Selecting a sample

The purpose for doing the survey and the context within which the results are to be used determine the depth and breadth of the sample taken. An overview, akin to a total body scan, would be a typical first step. Any shadow areas uncovered would warrant follow-up diagnosis: focusing the camera's lens on a particular part of the body.

The Board of the Nalle Clinic convened the 13 December 1984 retreat. Their purpose was to consider changes that could profoundly impact the Clinic. To make and implement big decisions without at least taking the pulse of the organisation would have been irresponsible patient care.

The pulse took the form of a climate survey, which 47 people responded to: influential physicians (28), including the entire Board and other formal and informal physician leaders; the most senior non-physician administrators (13), and a small number (6) of key technical support personnel (laboratory, X-ray technicians, and nursing supervisors). Those who completed the survey were invited to attend the retreat so they could share their own feelings and experiences. They put meat on the bones of the anonymous survey.

Format of the survey

The survey instrument focused on an inventory of specific behaviours known to be characteristic of organisations in search of excellence. The

---

[10] See pp. 35–37.

questionnaire measured several dimensions,[11] including *responsibility* (the extent to which individuals are accountable for their own job performance), *excellence* (the extent to which individuals are committed to producing quality work), and *team spirit* (the extent to which individuals support one another personally and professionally).

The respondents were asked to share their perceptions about the specific behaviours from three perspectives:

(A) Awareness of importance

An organisation's values are the core—the heart and soul—of its climate. The first perspective focused upon the extent of people's cognitive awareness of the importance of each behaviour to the achievement of organisational excellence. In excellence-oriented climates people agree on what it takes to deliver quality patient-centred care.

(B) Behavioural frequency

In a win-win organisation, management leads by example, aligning its own behaviour with organisational values. The second perspective focused upon the frequency of each behaviour in people's day-to-day experience. Excellence-oriented climates strive to "walk their talk", to minimise discrepancies between what they say and what they do.

(C) Consequences of occurrence

Continuous learning from experience is key to the search for excellence. Without constant feedback and encouragement, learning from experience cannot take place. The third perspective focused upon the consequences—formal and/or informal—that would be expected by persons if, and when, they exhibited each of the behaviours.

The quantitative scales used are reproduced below.

(A) Awareness of importance

You are being asked for your *personal perception* or belief about the extent to which the behaviour would be expected to contribute to organisational excellence at the Nalle Clinic. (Ignore, on this

---

[11] The current version of the climate survey measures 7 dimensions via 84 quantitative and 5 qualitative questionnaire items.

scale, whether or not you perceive the behaviour to exist at the Nalle Clinic.)

1	2	3	4	5	6	7
Major hindrance This behaviour cannot help us at all in achieving excellence			*Neutral* No impact one way or another			*Critical positive impact* Without this behaviour, achieving excellence will be doubtful

(B) Behavioural frequency

Next, review the same item of behaviour from the perspective of the extent to which, *in your personal experience*, you see each behaviour reflected at the Nalle Clinic. (Ignore on this scale any beliefs you may have about the importance of the behaviour in producing excellence or the consequences of the behaviour.)

1	2	3	4	5	6	7
I hardly ever see any indications of this behaviour being exhibited			I see indications of this behaviour exhibited on somewhat frequent basis			I see indications of this behaviour exhibited almost on a daily basis

(C) Consequences of occurrence

Next, review the same item of behaviour from the perspective of *your perception* of the consequences—formal and/or informal— which would be expected by the person(s) who exhibit(s) the behaviour.

1	2	3	4	5	6	7
This behaviour would be discouraged			This behaviour would receive no clear encouragement or discouragement			This behaviour would be clearly encouraged

Feeding back the survey results

Several anonymous feedback summaries were prepared. Each focused on a different facet of the X-ray. Subgroup summaries allowed a comparison of how different groups experienced the climate, for example, non-physician administrators and the physician Board. By examining the variance in perceptions (as distinct from the mean scores), among the members of a specific subgroup, inferences could be made as to the tightness versus looseness of various subcultures. For example, a department whose members pooled and shared equally all income could be expected, over time, to develop a highly consensual picture of the climate in their department. Regardless of the mean score on any particular climate dimension, this subsample could be expected to reflect high agreement (low variance). In contrast, a department whose members, for whatever reasons, were more loosely connected might reflect wider variances in perceptions.

I do not imply that tightness is better than looseness. Perceptual similarities may minimise conflicts and increase the possibility of group think. On the other hand, a diversity of perspectives can add richness and creativity as long as a common mission provides focus. Conducting surveys and discussing their results provides a valuable opportunity to manage the organisation's climate.

Individuals kept copies of their own responses so they could compare their perceptions with the anonymous group summaries. Individuals were free to share their personal perceptions, and many chose to do so during small subgroup discussions. Such willingness and openness are important signs that the patient-organisation is beginning to take responsibility for its own growth.

Reading the X-ray

The reading of an organisational climate survey, like reading a patient's X-ray, requires a delicate combination of science and art. Both are examined from many perspectives. Interpretation requires the active involvement of the human organism being diagnosed. Before treatment can begin, first impressions and intuitive hunches must be followed by deeper probing and more extensive diagnoses.

To acknowledge these realities and to ensure the patient's right to privacy, I will present and discuss only examples of surface-level, overall patterns (N = 47).

This sample of key individuals was very aware of (average mean scores almost a perfect 7), and in very high agreement about (low standard deviations), the importance of the following example behavioural patterns:

- setting high, but achievable, goals
- taking time to praise people when they did something well
- trusting people to do their jobs (versus watching over their shoulders all the time)

- looking for the cause of a problem when a mistake was made and learning from it (versus seeking to place the blame on a person).

At the other end of the scale, there was a typical lower mean score (slightly over 4) and high level of disagreement (standard deviation in excess of 1.5) on the issue of "exceeding the limits of one's formal authority when necessary to get the job done". As would be expected of an organisation in Stage I, a fraternity stage of development, the Board (physician-keepers of the Brotherhood) and the non-physician administrators were at opposite ends of this bell-shaped curve.

Commandments from on high may be set in stone, but life in the trenches requires trust and flexibility. The formal organisation will specify the job to be done, and then the informal organisation will determine how it actually gets done. Ironically, as a board member, a physician might agree to certain behaviour guidelines, but as a practitioner, exceed these limits. This inconsistency, born of privileged status, frustrates non-physician administrators.

By and large, the values that the Nalle Clinic agreed were important to the achievement of excellence indicated a healthy heart and soul. The patient-organisation, from my own experience, reflected a healthy level of conscious awareness.

Their *normal* developmental challenge—and I cannot stress enough their normality as a Stage-I organisation—was to bring their day-to-day behaviour into alignment with their conscious awareness of important values. The search for excellence is a never-ending journey, a process. Each plateau of achievement merely provides the sanctuary for a brief rest and the opportunity to learn from past experience.

On the basis of this assessment, Dr. Fernandez activates immediate, short-term therapies: he brings new blood on board. He authorises new committees to focus healing energies on "the various tasks necessary to provide strong leadership in the Clinic". The patient and the provider collaborate to determine these tasks. Dr. Fernandez appropriately emphasises the vision of a healthier future as well as the absence of guarantees and quick fixes.

It is important to emphasise that the map is not the territory. A climate survey, like an X-ray, can only suggest areas needing attention. Formal reward systems, clear value-driven mission statements, simple structures, informal pats on the back, heavy investments in training and development—these are ingredients essential for the creation of excellence-oriented organisational climates. All of these ingredients are necessary.

The organisation is a patient whose chief complaint and presenting illness reflect normal growing pains. It wanted to grow beyond its childhood (condominium) orientation. As its leader, Dr. Fernandez reports in his 13 December 1984, chart entry that senior management had demonstrated its verbal commitment to organisational cultural change. This chart entry itself is one example of how senior management dealt with individuals in the Clinic: management provided information about what the organisational cultural change might involve and gave people the freedom to choose to go through the process. Both physicians and non-physicians in senior management had already freely committed themselves to the cultural change, and in the final section of the 13 December 1984, memo, many of them enthusiastically stated their reasons.

This memo also serves as a new social contract, announcing to the Clinic that from now on, senior management's behaviour will be different and that it will serve as the example for the rest of the Clinic to follow:

> The Board of Directors is restructuring the entire administrative team and has appointed a new chief executive officer.... The Board will also authorise new committees to handle the various tasks necessary to provide strong leadership in the Clinic.... The Board will ask employees to participate in more task forces to help deal with specific problems. Our supervisors will take on new and greater responsibilities.... We will ask all in the organisation to elevate their standards of performance. Together, we can push one another to move the Clinic forward.

Anonymous questionnaires have described the realities that members of the Clinic observe and the ideals they desire. Senior management has accepted responsibility for the dissatisfactions the questionnaires revealed. The questionnaires also revealed readiness, motivation, and ability to change. As the memo stated, "Most employees aspire to quite high standards, and in some cases they expect more of themselves than those in leadership do".

Dr. Fernandez closes the body of this memo by reiterating senior management's commitment to organisational cultural change, to making the Clinic "the pre-eminent health-care organisation in this region". Developmentally, I associate such a mission statement with a Stage-III organisation in search of excellence. As I have noted, the operating psychological contract for such a Stage-III organisation

> is unique and very expensive. The organisation provides security from arbitrary layoffs, but not from dismissal for continued unacceptable performance. It also provides regular opportunities for

challenge, autonomy, and synergy. In return, individual members are expected to give up a piece of their *souls*—to invest of their *selves* in the business.

Once we've made a painful decision, we have a natural tendency to hope, if not act as though, we can detour around, or speed up, the steps the decision requires. Although its mission statement points to Stage III, the Nalle Clinic (and others like it) cannot avoid going through Stage II, which provides the training ground, the toughening up, necessary to move to Stage III.

Continuing his practice of organisational healing, Dr. Fernandez begins his 27 January 1985, chart entry with updates to the patient: he describes actions he committed management to at the close of the 13 December 1984, retreat. Both openness of information—central to informed consent—and reliability in meeting commitments—central to developing trust—are essential to a successful doctor-patient relationship. Senior management commits to taking concrete action to support cultural change: beyond their written mission statement, they promise to provide leadership, training, and money to those who will plan for and implement the cultural change. Dr. Fernandez makes careful and extensive use of teams—task-force cells—as skeletal reinforcements to stabilise a human organism struggling to maintain its balance in the face of intense but normal growing pains. He mobilises twelve such ad-hoc committees to treat the nineteen separate areas that need improvement.

Growing up, Dr. Fernandez notes, will require an approach to management that is "a distinct departure from past methods of making decisions about problems. The quality of our decisions should improve dramatically. The result of this effort should be a more integrated clinic where all personnel will more clearly comprehend their roles in the organisation and will, therefore, be able to make more significant contributions".

Organisationally, growing up means all parts of the body must take a larger share of personal responsibility to keep the entire organisation strong. "Every role is critical to the success of the organisation". Dr. Fernandez informs the patient once again that its full "participation is essential to the overall success of our mission".

The words *every role is critical* and *our mission* are vital to leadership in organisational cultural change. The mission statement is the entire Nalle Clinic's, by direction of the Board of Directors; yet it is individuals who act as leaders. Whether or not these initiatives are mutually beneficial, and at what costs to whom, depend on the quality of the exchange. The quality of the partnership, the relationship between a patient and a provider, determines the outcome of healing.

Creating the necessary win-win results depends on strong interpersonal skills, courage, and persistence. The preceding memos allow us to analyse Dr. Fernandez's style of communication, *how* he communicates what he says he is going to do, and what the patient needs to do. A physician-CEO's style of communication is crucial to influencing the patient-organisation to fulfil its part of the leadership transaction.

There are many useful programmes for developing communication skills. The model I use is from my course The *ABCs of Win-Win Relationships*. In all of our human interactions, we use our energies either to *push* thoughts, feelings, or ideas towards someone or to *pull* thoughts, feelings, or ideas from someone. When we *push* to shape and direct others' thinking and behaviours, we can use four styles: focusing on facts and logic, we *describe* what has happened in the past or is happening at the moment, and we *prescribe* what could or should happen in the future; focusing on our feelings, we *appreciate* the significance and value of what has happened in the past or is happening at the moment, and we *inspire* others to work together to achieve common goals.

When we *pull* from others, we also use four styles. Our first responsibility is to *attend*, to make sure we are receptive to what others *push*. Whether we agree or disagree with what others *push*, when we *ask* for their thoughts, feelings, or ideas, we must keep an open mind. We use a variety of verbal and non-verbal cues to communicate that we *understand* others' thoughts and ideas. When we sense and acknowledge others' feelings, we *empathise*.

These samples of his public communiqués demonstrate a balanced push-pull pattern.

Let us look more closely at Dr. Fernandez's 13December 1984, memo. After clearly and candidly *describing* what happened at the first retreat (including the dirty laundry), Dr. Fernandez *prescribes* the future implications: "In short, we will ask all in the organisation to elevate their standards of performance". He immediately follows this new expectation with an *inspirational* reminder of the power of teamwork: "Together we can push one another to move the Clinic forward".

Such a tall order is bound to stir up anxiety, resistance, and cynicism. Dr. Fernandez then shifts to communicating an understanding of, and *empathy* with, his patient: "None of these changes will be easy, simple, or quick. Some of them will be hard for some people to accept. Many of us have grown comfortable in our current roles and would rather not strive for higher levels of performance".

While not denying the validity of these feelings, Dr. Fernandez is careful to *appreciate* past achievements and current strengths: "However, with the commitment that so many physicians and employees have already shown", the "many smart, dedicated people committed to the project will not", he *prescribes*, "let it fizzle". He follows with further *inspiration*: "A new, shared sense of our commitment to be the pre-eminent health-care organisation in this region will be our motivation. This shared sense of mission will convert us from a loosely associated group of individual practitioners into a real organisation, in the grandest sense of the word".

Not everyone will agree with Dr. Fernandez's vision. He *asks* his patient to seek second and third opinions and to keep an open mind: "We invite you to contact any of these people [retreat attendees who publicly aired their own feelings along with Dr. Fernandez] and solicit their further comments".

Dr. Fernandez uses the tools of persistence: *descriptive* data, *prescriptive* recommendations, *appreciative* judgements, and *inspired* visions. He's equally determined to honourably discharge his persistent responsibilities, to stay in close, human touch with his patient. He remains patiently *attentive*, *asks* for counsel, expresses *understanding* of diverse concerns, and demonstrates *empathy*.

Leadership in organisational culture change, as previously noted, requires the flexible and humane application, based upon valid diagnoses, of generic healing therapies. Quick-fix formulas will not result in permanent healing. Each treatment plan must be tailored to the specific and evolving needs of the patient-organisation. My commentary on the initial treatment plan developed by Dr. Fernandez and the Nalle Clinic will, therefore, take the form of a series of questions. These questions will serve as a checklist of issues to be addressed by physician-CEOs and their patient organisations to determine their readiness, motivation, and ability to journey in search of excellence.

1. Mission question: "Has the creation of the required agreed-upon mission statement been the result of an extensive group process?"

Many organisations begin to sink themselves by avoiding the very painful and time-consuming requirement to agree together on "where we are going". They delegate this responsibility to one (their physician-CEO) or to a small handful of individuals.

The irony of this trap is that the quality of the resulting statement, in terms of the words on paper, may be identical to that which might result from an expensive and gut-wrenching process among a broadly based group. Since the quality of the process is as important as the final content, skipping the process guarantees two potential deadly outcomes, both related to commitment. Let's look at these one at a time.

The first potential problem is the lack of psychological ownership of change. The famous Western Electric "Hawthorne effect" experiments verified what our common sense always knew: when you want to make a change, you have to involve the people who will be changing. Let them help plan and implement the ideas. The same principle applies to the Nalle Clinic: involve the physician-CEO, the Board of Directors, and the senior executives. Put them in a room and let them hash out a mission statement together. Then the words of the mission statement can come to life because many people agree on them and want them to succeed.

The second potential problem is the lack of continuity of change. Another advantage of having several people work on the mission statement is that they are less likely to make inappropriate, and potentially dangerous, wholesale changes: to throw out the baby with the bath water. Past successes, like a child's favourite toy, can ease the pain of moving to a new plateau of excellence. Many treasured and essential learnings occurred as an organisation arrived at its current state of development. Some pieces of its proud history will be critical to keep on board as its new journey begins.

2. Structure question: "Have temporary life-support structures been established to help people cope with the early stages of transition?"

The growing-up process requires us to release familiar, old patterns and to face new challenges. Like a patient who has just endured open-heart surgery, an organisation embarking on a journey towards wellness will need temporary structures to ease the transition, particularly because it's travelling into uncharted territory.

The organisation's vital signs must be checked frequently. Management by walking around and regular, loosely structured group meetings are the keys to checking its pulse. Managers will know how everyone's doing, how everyone's handling the normal and expected anxiety in times of change. Holding the patient's hand also ensures that complications can be diagnosed and treated early.

These will not be easy steps to take. Human nature being what it is, those seen as responsible for the patient-organisation's stress and anxiety will not always be greeted with open arms. It will be tempting for them to stay in the office, hiding behind mountains of paperwork, in order to avoid hostility. But it's essential to stay in touch.

3. Procedures question: "Are enough tools available to ensure that individuals are ready, willing, and able to support the mission?"

Most organisations *severely underestimate* what is required to support behavioural changes during major transitions. People must develop new habits and unlearn some old ones. They must develop teamwork.

A Stage-I organisation is like a baseball team. While some players may be gifted enough to play more than one position—shortstop and second base, for example—most players specialise. Baseball's fundamental nature is low, on-line interdependence. Except for the occasional fly ball, it takes pairs (pitcher and catcher) or trios (infielder, first baseman, and catcher, as a backup) to play the game: to throw and catch and tag the runner out.

A Stage-II organisation is more like a football team. The quarterback calls the play, and *in theory*, it will be successful *if* all eleven players perform their roles perfectly. Compared to baseball, football is characterised by higher levels of on-line interdependence. While players specialise, they need other skills, too: a tackle might also intercept the ball and run for a touchdown. A Yankees player who tries out for the Miami Dolphins will need dramatically different teamwork muscles. The Bo Jacksons of the world are rare.

Finally, a Stage-III organisation is like a basketball team, which uses very few pre-set plays. While skilled players are necessary, teamwork is even more important in this highly interdependent game. Teamwork means practising together under game conditions long enough and hard enough to be able, as Bill Russell once commented, to see the play developing "in slow motion" and know "intuitively" where a team-mate will be in the next split second.

While numbers are impossible to specify, it is safe to say that an organisation can *not* earmark too much time and money for training budgets. Before pushing off on its journey into uncharted waters, an organisation must stash skilled training resources on board.

4. The question of intangibles: "Do you have faith in your mission and belief in yourself?"

The last factor on the treatment-plan checklist will ultimately determine the journey's success or failure; yet it will be impossible to assess before the fact. Just as medicine can bring unprecedented knowledge, skill, and technology to a patient's care, it is often the patient's spiritual will to live that tips the scales of the healing process. Similarly, other people and events—a family intervention or a car crash—might bring an alcoholic into A.A., but the programme of growing up will succeed only if the alcoholic accepts an underlying faith in a higher-order God and believes, heart and soul, that he or she is doing God's will.

As health-care organisations and their physician leaders move through their stages of development, their underlying reasons for embarking on these journeys will be severely tested and retested. This will be particularly true of those who dare to venture out of Stage II and make the quantum leap required to sail to a new world. Those who are successful will be driven by a belief that excellence in patient-centred care will be best delivered by self-actualising organisations. Organisational culture change—the continuous process of growing up—is fundamentally a self-help, self-healing programme.

In closing his 1 February 1985 chart entry, Dr. Fernandez expresses cautious optimism concerning the success of the self-help relationship between himself and his patient, the Nalle Clinic: "I sense an understanding that things are happening ... I think we will win their support".

Physician leaders, like Dr. Fernandez, will experience dramatic transformations in their self-images. They will have to surrender their deeply ingrained roles as the primary providers of quality care in patient treatment. In its place they will have to "grow up", to treat entire organisations of providers as patients in need of quality care. Such transformational journeys will trigger predictable psychological and behavioural dynamics.

In Part Three, we move from 1 February 1985 to 5 December 1988. During that period, Dr. Fernandez and I met a dozen times and spoke by phone many more times. Many of our conversations had to do with quality care and leadership, and the differences, if any, between the two. During one conversation, I asked Dr. Fernandez to describe the feelings of being CEO of an organisation evolving out of its medical-condominium orientation.

What follows is Dr. Fernandez's account of how leading such a mission feels. He gives us his personal perspective on the process of leadership and organisational cultural change, almost four years to the day since he formally accepted the role as chief provider of the care team responsible for the Nalle Clinic.

Part Three

Progress report

Dr. Raymond Fernandez's personal chart entry

Edited transcript of an audiotape sent to Irv Rubin

5 December 1988

IN MAKING THE transition from physician to medical director and CEO, I crossed the invisible line between being us and being *them*. I remain sensitive to this distinction, and others cite it when it seems to serve their purposes. No matter how hard the physicians try to cover up their feelings, to them I am clearly a traitor. Understanding the psychodynamics of the situation does not ease the pain of having one of my close colleagues reject me because of my new role.

Although I had no difficulty logically seeing the need to give up my established practice, with which I had become very comfortable, announcing and making the necessary split was not easy to do. Telling my patients and my peers that I had decided to leave them was emotionally trying, particularly with members in my call group. They considered me disloyal, a traitor, because their lives would immediately become more difficult: they would have to tighten their belts to take more nights on call. Their career plans were entwined with mine, and now I had unilaterally decided to desert them. The way I felt I needed to behave for the greater good of the organisation would, I know, leave some feeling that I had put other interests ahead of theirs. Thus, they became intent on discouraging me from carrying out my intentions.

Initially, I tried to strike a compromise by keeping one foot in my practice and one in administration. I even tried maintaining the old call schedule for a while. But before long, I realised that this compromise was not workable. I was being unfair to my family, my patients, my peers, and myself. I would have to leave behind the financial and emotional security I had built over several years in my practice.

One doesn't usually leave one comfortable situation for another situation unless the second one seems quite clearly dependable. In my case, I could not depend on my peers to support my decision to move to administration. I had no role models there to welcome me or serve as advisors. The only advice I was getting from those I had grown to trust was not to make the change. To convince myself that those around me didn't understand the situation well enough to give me good long-term advice, that I would have to make my decision without any encouragement, forced me to perceive myself in the role of a crusader. I was willing to sacrifice myself and my happiness to do something for my peers that they couldn't yet see was good for them, but that they would eventually appreciate. The situation was analogous to recommending a blood transfusion to a Jehovah's Witness. We know from our training and experience that the advice is good; we know that the patient is not able to accept that advice; but we feel we've got to give the advice anyway.

Realising that I had no formal training in business, leadership, management, or organisational psychology heightened my personal insecurity. The search committee were unable to give me a clear definition of the role they were asking me to assume. In fact, after they selected me, they asked me to write the original job description. They also asked me where I was going to get some management experience.

At this stage, I had to develop courage. With very little in the way of guidelines or advisors, I had to have the courage to make my own decisions about what was best for me and for the organisation. With no guidelines for measuring success or predicting the long-term consequences my decisions would have on me and the group, I had a strong fear of failure. And I recalled a lesson I had learned years earlier, when I first hypnotised my college roommate.

I had read a couple of books on hypnosis and had talked about it with my father, who used it in his medical practice. I felt that I had a pretty good grasp of the didactic basis for hypnotism. I presented myself to my roommate as "having a lot of experience". He wouldn't stop begging me to put him into a trance that would allow him to stop smoking and to study harder without distractions. When I finally agreed to hypnotise him, the ease with which I put him into a trance amazed me. And terrified me. What if I couldn't awaken him? What if I caused this poor fellow some type of harm? Why had I allowed myself even to try such a thing? Somehow I bluffed my way through and got him out of the trance. But the realisation of the responsibility that went along with that mysterious power remains a frightening, valuable lesson for me.

At this stage, I also had to learn to deal with isolation. In this organisational culture that had not had someone in a role of power and authority, physicians have trouble communicating with me. Their view of me as a traitor has shut off certain channels. They neither understand nor appreciate my new role, although they apparently sense that it is essential. I have a related problem with some of the administrators, because as CEO, I am now their boss. They, too, think a physician in an administrative role is a waste: administrators should administer, and physicians should treat patients. With no real peer group, I don't feel that I can let down my guard with anyone. While both groups clearly want me to succeed, they need to see me fail to prove their belief that physicians don't make good administrators.

I ask myself, "Can I do this job? Do I want this job?" I have the luxury of being able to go back to being a physician. On days when the aggravation becomes extreme, I remember how easy my job was when all I had to do was make simple life-and-death decisions for individual patients. But I remind myself that as a physician, I had to put my patient's needs before my own desires. Now, I have this same feeling of obligation to the organisation: my patient needs me.

However, the manager's role has significant differences. I don't see the results of a decision until some time after I've made it. Frequently, my colleagues ask me to tell them what they need to do, which sometimes translates into my telling them how to conduct their practice, but which they see as my telling them how to treat patients. This sort of conflict is ongoing. The frustration it creates seems pervasive, since most of the highly intelligent professionals I work with have little appreciation for the big picture I must see. They look only at their individual practices and their individual realities. One of my most important duties is to translate and communicate others' ideas. However, listeners tend to mistrust a translator they must depend on.

Rejection from my peers is painful. They seem to enjoy disagreeing openly with decisions I make. Disagreement with an individual decision tends to lead to loss of confidence in the competence and authority of my position. Any decision I make is bound to irritate at least ten percent of my constituents. However, no two decisions irritate the same ten percent, so by the time I have made ten decisions, I have irritated everyone. The fact that these peers are my equals in the medical culture makes functioning as the decision maker that much harder. I have difficulty accepting that I must accept ultimate blame for all failures in the organisation. So I constantly wonder if it's really worth it. Like the physician who has lost a patient or become embroiled in a lawsuit, I wonder if the anger and frustration I feel are worth the reward.

Organised medicine faces many challenges: do we need to circle the wagons, fight, give in, or learn to make friends with the new system? In the midst of this indecision, organisations ask the physician-manager to lead the troops down the right path. We see groups in our community succeeding in joint ventures with hospitals, while other groups ask us to lead the fight against "those damned hospital administrators". In the role of physician-executive, we are supposed to have a clear vision of what is best for our organisations and where to lead them. The simple truth is that we really don't know. Yet to keep our positions as effective leaders, we've got to keep telling our troops where we are taking them.

The other side of the story is that what I am doing now is fun. Having the power and autonomy of a decision maker is something to which I think most physicians naturally aspire. The highs are higher and the lows, lower in my current position than in medical practice. As patients literally put their lives in their physician's hands, so, too, the life of the organisation is in mine. The challenge of controlling a complex organisation's culture, financial performance, quality control, and morale is exciting. As the organisation progresses through change and growth, I take a parent's pride in its successes. Still, the fear and frustration of dealing with the unknown is something physician-managers have to live with every day. Like Columbus, we have to realise that most of the people actually hope we'll fall off the end of the world so that they can remain secure in their belief that the world is flat.

Commentary

Leading by example

Irwin Rubin, PhD

IN MANY WAYS the Nalle Clinic did not want to be led. Here the patient, not an individual but a collection of providers, rejects Dr. Fernandez. The birth of an extended self-image, one that admits collections of providers as one's patients, triggers deep, emotional reactions. We see Dr. Fernandez's hopes and fears in his December 1988 chart entry. "I am clearly a traitor," Dr. Fernandez says; yet he has no trouble understanding that the rejections are not personal. He is able to control the pain rather than avoid it.

Reacting to the imminent death of a part of his old self-image, his psyche begins to negotiate a series of devil's bargains. "Initially," Dr. Fernandez says, "I tried to strike a compromise by keeping one foot in my practice and one in administration." For someone of his integrity, such a compromise will be short lived. He quickly realises that this compromise is "unfair to my family, my patients, my peers, and myself".

Dr. Fernandez is caught between reference groups ("between being us and being *them*") and between self-images ("I am clearly a traitor"), without "financial and emotional security", without even the potential security of "a clear definition of the role [the search committee] were asking me to assume", and with peers "intent on discouraging me from carrying out my intentions". The intensity of these conflicting emotions calls for a more intense devil's bargain. When rational compromise does not work, psychological compromise becomes tempting. Trying such a compromise "in the role of a crusader ... willing to sacrifice myself and my happiness ... was analogous", Dr. Fernandez said, "to recommending a blood transfusion to a Jehovah's Witness". And with similar consequences.

By confronting and accepting what began as a "strong fear of failure", Dr. Fernandez uncovers an equally strong fear of success. Through a process Jung calls synchronicity, Dr. Fernandez recalls a lesson in humility from many years earlier, which began with his success in hypnotising a friend: "The ease with which I put him into a trance amazed me. And terrified me. What if I couldn't awaken him? [What if he died?] What if I caused this poor fellow [this entire organisation-as-patient] some type of harm?" As life and death are equal parts of the experience, so are healing and failing.

Psychic acceptance of aloneness and impermanence are keys to personal succession. (*Succession*, as I use the term here, is "the process of moving from one stage of development to another".) Paradoxically, increased openness and acceptance are the best defence against peers who consider Dr. Fernandez a traitor. "I also had to learn to deal with isolation.... While both groups clearly want me to succeed, they need to see me fail to prove their belief that physicians don't make good administrators". Increasing comfort in the fact that both administrators and physicians know that "as CEO, I am now their boss" does not relieve Dr. Fernandez's isolation, the loneliness at the top: "With no real peer group, I don't feel that I can let down my guard with anyone".

Self-doubt creeps into Dr. Fernandez's thoughts: "Can I do this job? ... But I remind myself that as a physician, I had to put my patient's needs before my own desires. Now, I have this same feeling of obligation to the organisation: my patient needs me". A new self-image is taking hold. Dr. Fernandez has to act, fully aware that the consequences will be far-reaching, but seldom universally good or desirable: "By the time I have made ten decisions, I have irritated everyone".

Only a special breed of physician can make the transition to physician-executive. And only a special breed of person in that position will acknowledge that, "In the role of physician-executive, we are supposed to have a clear vision of what is best for our organisations and where to lead them. The simple truth is that we really don't know. Yet to keep our positions as effective leaders, we've got to keep telling our troops where we are taking them". I'm pleased, although not surprised, to see that for such a person, Ray Fernandez, "The other side of the story is that what I am doing now is fun".

In the memo of 5 December 1988, the ambivalent forces of human nature seemed to be in a state of peaceful coexistence—fear of success balancing the capacity to succeed, but only temporarily. Succession is a never-ending process. From the high points we can draw strength and insight, which we will need to climb the next mountain. Growth was causing some of the same symptoms Dr. Fernandez noted four years earlier to reappear, along with some new ones. Conflict within the Nalle

Clinic over its control had become public record. The 15 January 1990, edition of the weekly *Business Journal* of Charlotte carried the headline "Nalle Lawsuit Vs. [a physician who left the Clinic to go out on his own, violating a contract he signed when he joined the Clinic] Heads to Appellate Court". The accompanying story stated, "The conflict with [the physician] isn't the first time Nalle has battled to enforce its restrictive covenant".

Five days later, the Charlotte *Observer* headlined, "Nalle Clinic Considers Taking on Financial Partner". According to the article, declining revenues, a result of the rapid growth and external environmental changes, led the patient to seek a new partner to "strengthen our financial position and assure our future". The report quoted Dr. Fernandez: "We had a bad third quarter. The fourth quarter was much improved. We need some capital. It's not a new need, and it's not an emergency need. It's not something we'd die without".

On March 1, 1990, the Nalle Clinic exercised its inalienable right to a second opinion. A process that had begun some five years earlier had come to its own unique conclusion. Under Dr. Fernandez's leadership, the Nalle Clinic had taken the steps necessary to move away from its condominium roots and to become a more mature business organisation. According to the March 5 Charlotte *Observer*, "Attempting to strengthen its finances and its future, the Nalle Clinic finalised a joint venture Thursday with PhyCor, a Nashville-based company that will manage the Clinic's business and provide money for expansion.... Under the agreement, [Dr.] Fernandez steps down as chief executive officer of the Clinic but remains medical director".

Knowledge without wisdom is useless. And wisdom is impossible without the courage to learn from experience. However hard we may try to control them, processes of human growth and development have a pace and a rhythm of their own. Part Four gives us a view of the human experience of death and dying as Dr. Fernandez struggles to accept the painful realisation that he is about to become the first past-physician-CEO of the Nalle Clinic. His goal five years earlier was to assist his patient to grow into a more business-like organisation. Unanticipated stresses caused the evolution to proceed at a pace that surprised everyone. Although this stage of development ended somewhat traumatically, Dr. Fernandez and his patient-organisation have achieved the results they wanted. He has discharged his leadership responsibilities, and his patient has discharged him.

Commentary

Reflections of a seasoned veteran

Henry Berman, MD
President and CEO of Group Health Northwest

T HE HISTORY OF the Nalle Clinic and of Dr. Raymond Fernandez's
struggles as its first physician-CEO is one that many group practices and physician managers have experienced in the past
decade. A number of changes in the environment have forced the profession to respond in ways that have led to experiences such as this one.
These changes include an increasing number of physicians, more competition from other health-care providers, more pressure from the government and employers for cost-containment, higher expectations from
patients, and a dramatic increase in the number of managed-care
organisations.

As Dr. Fernandez described in his introduction, from its founding in
1921, the Clinic had grown to 40 physicians by 1975 and then doubled
in size in less than 15 years. In response to environmental pressures,
many group practices follow this pattern. It is a way of dealing with
increased specialisation and competition and demands for efficiency,
and it enables the physicians to contract with HMOs and PPOs to protect or increase their patient base. However, many groups do not appreciate the importance of high-quality management in achieving their
ambitious goals. For others, this appreciation is primarily intellectual
until they hear the hard knocks of reality at their front doors. The Nalle
Clinic was no exception.

We can trace this problem back to its roots in the Clinic's decision to
make Dr. Fernandez its first medical director. In correspondence with
me, Dr. Fernandez says his honest assessment of that decision in 1980
is that, of the three candidates for the position, "the organisation found

me to be the least threatening". Dr. Fernandez describes himself as having no prior experience with medical management. Someone with a bit of experience might have recognised that he was encountering a Groucho Marx paradox: Groucho turned down membership in a country club, refusing to belong to any club that would accept him as a member. My point is that, despite having no management experience, Dr. Fernandez was chosen for the job; and an organisation that makes sure that it selects such a person is also going to make sure that that person cannot succeed.

Dr. Fernandez's correspondence with me also states that his "strongest skill was probably in being able to soothe troubled waters and look for areas of compromise rather than making dictatorial decisions". When group practices finally concede that they need a physician-manager, they typically choose a nice guy as their first medical director. Although strong interpersonal skills are necessary to be able to do this difficult job effectively, being too nice can be a liability.

We can find a useful analogy in styles of parenting. Authoritarian parents ("My way is the only way") eventually lose their ability to influence their children; authoritarian physician-CEOs fail much more quickly. Laissez-faire parents ("Do your own thing") are not very effective, but may well continue to have good interpersonal relationships with their children.[12] In my experience, laissez-faire physician-CEOs are not able to manage change in their organisations, yet this style is very popular. I believe that popularity may reflect the correct perception of how badly an authoritarian approach works out, coupled with a lack of understanding of what will work: the authoritative style. The authoritative style is not a compromise between the other two styles but a third, entirely different approach. Authoritative parents and leaders understand that they have knowledge and skills that are greater in certain areas, and responsibilities that they cannot shrug off. They also understand that wise leaders make most decisions after considerable consultation with those whom the decisions affect, that they hold as few decisions to themselves as possible, and that they encourage independent decision-making. Awareness of behavioural choices and their consequences plus the flexibility to respond to changing conditions are key. I do not believe that the Nalle Clinic was ready for an authoritative leader at that point in its history.

---

[12] *Editor's note:* A middle possibility exists here: reactive parents ("I'll do whatever makes you happy"), who quickly discover that their children do not know their own wants.

Another warning sign occurred when the Board "did not spell out the position's power and authority". The Clinic also lacked a formal goal-setting process and had never undertaken an evaluation of its leaders. In my experience, these shortcomings are also typical but a real danger to physician-executives. Our jobs are always complex, with many different groups to please, and, inevitably, displease. Setting goals flushes out the issues, and undergoing evaluation against those goals not only provides useful feedback to the physician-executive and the board but also protects the physician-executive against sudden shifts in the wind. Not having goals and an evaluation is similar to a physician's treating a patient with no plan and with no interest in measuring the success of the treatment.

On the other hand, as Irv Rubin points out, one real plus was the Clinic's realisation that Dr. Fernandez would need training to be able to do his job effectively. Dr. Fernandez's ability to learn mainly from his mistakes is reassuring to the rest of us who have had the same experience. When I am very lucky, I learn from someone else's mistakes. More often, I learn from my own. Mediocre managers are not people who do not make mistakes, but those who do not learn from them. Experience is not the best teacher if no learning takes place.

The next key moment in this story occurred when Dr. Fernandez increased his time to 85 percent administrative and went off call. "The Board readily agreed" to his suggestion, but others—in particular, those he shared call with—apparently did not. I don't know what process, if any, the Board used to make this decision, but they would have done well at this point to get buy-in from the entire physician group. I doubt that the statement "We all realised that my primary role had changed from being a clinician to being an administrator" is complete. Even though physicians in larger groups elect a board and supposedly delegate authority to that group, they seldom completely accept the fact that they have empowered that group to make certain decisions, usually those involving power or money or symbolically important issues. I have found no substitute for one-on-one or small-group discussions with the front-line physicians before making such decisions.

One such important symbolic issue is call. Sometimes it is a real issue as well, and the physicians left in the call schedule have to shoulder a heavy burden. But more often, that situation is not the problem, even when people act as if it is. They think, "Real doctors take call. Being a part-time administrator is all right, as long as you continue doing everything a real doctor does". Even though such an arrangement is neither sensible nor possible, physicians seem to be able to pretend that it is.

Starting without a firm foundation (the aforementioned Groucho Marx paradox) and moving forward into being an administrator without full support of the physicians left Dr. Fernandez in a precarious position in late 1984 when the Board asked him to become its first CEO. This was probably his last, best chance to clarify his authority, establish formal goals, develop an evaluation process, and put all these in writing in a formal contract.

One key phrase from the 13 December 1984, memo highlights the problem Dr. Fernandez faced: "The Board of Directors is restructuring the entire administrative team and has appointed Dr. Fernandez to quarterback the team as chief executive officer". The CEO should be the general manager or coach, not the quarterback. Even quarterbacks who call their own plays in the huddle—a rare and vanishing breed, to be sure—do so in the context of an overall game plan worked out by general management. The memo has already pointed out the fact that physicians caused many of the problems by making decisions that were good for them rather than good for the organisation, as well as by protecting their own divisions at the expense of others'. These behaviours and attitudes, common in group practices, are among the most difficult issues to deal with effectively. The only hope a physician-manager has, to be able to make necessary changes, is to have the authority to make controversial decisions, not to be someone who just executes decisions others make.

The mission statement is worthy of discussion. Excellence-oriented, patient-centred mission statements are very much in vogue these days. The Nalle Clinic's rhetoric is impressive, but does it express what the physicians really wanted? Or did they want to be a more successful business, to have a better billing system and more capital, to earn more money? At this point, the Clinic is a classic Stage-I organisation. Does it really want to leap to Stage III? Does it want to be a more successful Stage-I organisation? Or does it want to move to Stage II? Aligning words and deeds is one of the leadership challenges.

Stage-I organisations are unable to deal with conflict in a healthy way. Instead of being impressed that those attending the January 1985 planning retreat specified nineteen separate areas in need of improvement, I would have been concerned that this might have represented pseudo-agreement, one way to avoid dealing with conflict. The group's coming up with nineteen areas for improvement makes me think of patients who see the light and agree to stop smoking and drinking and start exercising and dieting, all at the same time. Saying you will change everything ends up no different from deciding to change nothing. The most difficult task for a patient, or an organisation, is to change *any-thing*. Coming up with a list of nineteen areas needing change is a first step. Choosing the priority need among them and making the change permanent is the giant step.

Landscape architects use the phrase "respect the genius of the place". They do not try to turn a desert home into a piece of England. The Clinic might have had better success trying to become the best Stage-I organisation possible—and, in the process, starting inevitably on the path to Stage II, an effective business, rather than remaining a fraternity. Irv Rubin's commentary notes the organisation's desire to skip the difficult process of going first to Stage II on the way to Stage III. I agree that thinking this jump is possible is an easy mistake to make since one wishes fervently that it were possible. It is no more possible than a child's becoming an adult without going through adolescence.

In Part Three, Dr. Fernandez provides unusual insight into how being a physician-executive feels. Because he wrote the notes a year before the most serious new developmental challenges became apparent, their insights are fresher than those we might develop in retrospect. Dealing with change means dealing with loss, and Elizabeth Kubler-Ross's model is useful in understanding the stages all of us go through when we experience change. For example, in dealing with the issue of giving up call, Dr. Fernandez experiences *denial* ("Everyone agreed that it was necessary"), *anger* ("They considered me a traitor"), *bargaining* ("I even tried maintaining the old call schedule for a while"), *sadness*, and *acceptance* ("I would have to leave behind the financial and emotional security I had built").

Dr. Fernandez's honesty in describing his isolation and fear of failure is unusual. Most of the time we are busy fooling others, no doubt in order to fool ourselves. Dr. Fernandez also expresses poignantly the loneliness of a CEO ("I could not depend on my peers.... I had no role models to welcome me.... The only advice I was getting ... was not to make the change"). As lonely as being CEO is for anyone, it is even more difficult for physician-CEOs in their first such position. Non-physician CEOs reach their positions after years of moving up an organisation's ladder. Over the years, their peer group changes in a series of successive stages. As CEOs, their peers become CEOs they have come to know from similar organisations. But the physician-CEO must make the jump all at once, from a highly collegial relationship with dozens of physicians to a position with few, if any, role models, and no support systems. Like divers with no opportunity for decompression and re-acclimation, physician-CEOs find that too rapid a rise to the top can cause emotional disorientation and physical pain.

Dr. Fernandez's fear of failure is another common experience for physician-executives. By the time we have reached such a position, we have been involved in medicine for at least 15 years, often many more. We have a set of valuable skills that we can depend on, gratifying relationships with a large number of patients, a positive self-image, and the closest thing to a guaranteed ability to make a comfortable living that our society has to offer. Suddenly we find ourselves in a position with little or no training and little or no confidence in our skills, cut off from grateful patients and companionable colleagues, and at risk of being out of a job on short notice. Fear of failure represents a rational assessment of a difficult situation, not a panic response.

Dr. Fernandez also describes his difficulties gaining acceptance from the other administrators, who resented his being their leader despite, and perhaps because of, his apparent lack of qualifications. In my experience, these administrators are easier to win over than the many physicians who resent the power and authority of the physician-executive. Acknowledging their expertise and your own deficiencies and asking for their help are critical and are not, as might be initially feared, at all inconsistent with the authoritative style recommended earlier. Confidence and strength are required to know and own one's limitations. Since people expect physicians to be egotists, a bit of honest humility goes a long way, especially when the truth of such an attitude is so apparent. In order to succeed as a CEO of any organisation, one must work effectively with senior managers. An additional benefit of working closely with one's senior staff is the likelihood that an open, trusting relationship with this group will become one of the few opportunities the physician-executive can count on for positive interpersonal experiences within the organisation.

At the close of Part Three, Dr. Fernandez discusses three of the special challenges physician-executives face: the lack of immediate feedback on the results of decisions, the impossibility of pleasing all physicians at all times, and the uncertainty inherent in many management decisions. An additional concern that he describes may be easier to avoid: the belief that "I must accept ultimate blame for all the failures in the organisation". Although CEOs must, of course, be willing to accept responsibility for all failures, they are hardly at fault, any more than they would be responsible for all successes. The recommendation to work closely with a highly effective senior-management team is the best antidote to feeling so overwhelmingly responsible.

We cannot avoid the other three problems, only understand them. Being a physician-CEO, particularly in an organisation as fundamentally strong as the Nalle Clinic, is not so much like being a physician for a sick patient as it is like providing anticipatory guidance or health-maintenance advice to a patient experiencing normal growing pains. The rewards of preventive medicine are also in the distant future and require the physician's unwavering belief that the efforts are worthwhile in the absence of observable results. Dr. Fernandez's profound statement that "by the time I have made ten decisions, I have irritated everyone" shows that black humour, long an ally of physicians who need to learn to deal with death, is equally helpful to the physician-executive. This experience must be particularly difficult for someone like Dr. Fernandez, who believes that his "strongest skill was probably in being able to soothe troubled waters".

Finally, a CEO must deal with uncertainty. The reality of most senior-management decisions is that someone has already made the easy ones by the time an issue comes to your attention. You must use inadequate data for a much higher percentage of these decisions than in your experience as a physician. The ability to manage ambiguity and uncertainty is a critical quality for successful CEOs. However, in light of his statement that "we've got to keep telling our troops where we are taking them", the medical model may be hurting Dr. Fernandez. At times, if physicians fairly present alternatives and the risks and benefits of the approaches they choose, they may assure patients that a treatment will work out for the best even if they are less certain than that. This false certainty is seldom a useful approach for a CEO, particularly so in organisations driven by physicians who, as was noted earlier, are among the most difficult patients to manage.

Some of the openness and honesty with the physicians that Irv Rubin recommends in his first commentary on this section can be helpful. Paradoxically, when CEOs admit that they are uncertain about the best course to take, the effect can be to energise other staff—in this case, physicians in particular—to take more responsibility for decision-making, thereby decreasing their feelings of unhealthy dependency. This effect also precludes others from punishing the CEO for so-called failure (the only real failure is not learning from our experiences), since many people are involved.

We can hardly consider the experiences of the Nalle Clinic and Dr. Fernandez as failures. Their patients received good care. The organisation grew and changed. Dr. Fernandez knows much more about management than he did ten years ago. And thanks to his generously describing these experiences, so do the rest of us. Stage-I physician-organisations all over the country have repeated the Clinic's story for the past decade and will continue to do so for another decade, as more and more of them evolve into successful Stage-II organisations in order to survive in an increasingly complex environment. The best of these will go on to excellence, to Stage III.

To help ourselves in this evolution, we must learn what we can from the teaching moments available to us, and this case gives us such an opportunity. A review of Dr. Fernandez's comments shows a recurrent theme. At various times he feels

- like a physician treating a Jehovah's Witness, knowing "that the patient is not able to accept advice, but we feel we've got to give the advice anyway";
- like Columbus: "most people actually hope we'll fall off the end of the world"; and
- like a general "having to order some of his troops to storm a hill, absolutely knowing full well in advance that a lot of them are going to get shot and killed".[13]

Family therapists talk of "the identified patient", who commonly turns out to be the member of the family who is the most sensitive and intuitive and who acts out the family's unconscious wishes. Dr. Fernandez assumed this role for the Nalle Clinic. He describes himself as being a translator and a communicator. He sees the Board choosing him because of his lack of experience, because they could trust him not to upset the apple cart. His metaphors all deal with failure and loss and seem to represent what the Clinic needed of its leader during that period of its evolution.

A number of health-policy experts believe that group practices are the kind of medical organisation in the best position to take advantage of the changes that are occurring in the business of providing and financing health care in the United States at this time. But to fulfil this role, these physician-led organisations will need to choose as their leaders those who they hope will succeed, not those whom they can count on to fulfil their unconscious need to resist change. Physician-managers who have gone through the kind of trial by fire that Dr. Fernandez has experienced and who have learned as much as he has will be ideal candidates for positions of leadership in organisations striving for excellence.

---

[13] The quotation is from a tape dictated after the announcement of the Clinic's merger with PhyCor. See p. 115 for the text.

Commentary

Feelings in transition

Kevin Sullivan, MD
Vice President of Medical Affairs, Port Huron Hospital

WHILE READING a draft of this manuscript by Raymond Fernandez and Irv Rubin, I realised how little I had read about the feelings that accompany the transition to the role of physician-executive. Dr. Fernandez's open discussion (in Part Three) of his feelings as a physician-CEO encouraged me to express to him and to the reader some of the feelings that anyone is likely to encounter in making this journey into administration from the private practice of medicine.

Before deciding on a career as a physician-executive, you need to take a gut check of some important feelings. As a potential physician-executive, you must genuinely like and respect both physicians and administrators. Caring about the professional values and feelings of both will allow you to provide a buffer between them and to aid their communication with one another. If you are impatient or you hate meetings and paperwork, look for your career elsewhere. If you have a strong need to be in control, you feel uncomfortable working in teams, or you feel that consensus building is a waste of time, you will find most physician-executive positions frustrating. When physicians ask me whether they should consider careers as physician-executives, I take them through this gut check. The majority offer me condolences and say, "Thank God, I am a doctor".

But for some, like Dr. Fernandez, the challenge is right, and a whole new set of feelings surfaces. The importance and intensity of these feelings will vary by individual and by circumstances. A major feeling to deal with is that you have abandoned your patients, colleagues, and clinical practice. Dr. Fernandez felt this acutely: "Telling my patients and my peers that I had decided to leave them was emotionally trying, particularly with members of my call group". Both patients and colleagues want you and need you to care for them; colleagues need you to share call with them and be available for consultation. I did not feel right about becoming a full-time physician-executive until I had recruited my replacement to see my patients and to share call with my partner. At times when my patients say they wish I were still in practice, I wonder what the contract is that develops between physician and patient. "How can you give up all that residency training?" my father asked me. Not an easy question to answer. How do I explain walking away from skills I learned in four years of residency and strengthened in seventeen years of private practice? Overcoming feelings of guilt and selfishness related to abandonment requires a strong commitment to the new vision and values of a Stage-III organisation.

Another prevalent feeling is fear of the unknown. As Dr. Fernandez clearly articulated, the role of the physician-executive is to "have a clear vision of what is best for our organisations and where to lead them". Inevitably, you ask yourself, "Can I really make a difference in the organisation by taking on this role? What if they don't like me and fire me? Can I afford to leave the financial security of private practice? Am I doing this for the right reasons, or am I just running away from the problems of private practice? Will I be happy and fulfilled in this new role?" To neutralise some of the fear of the unknown, I started as a part-time medical director. But ultimately, you have to take the plunge and live the answers. Dr. Fernandez correctly points out that you can't do justice to either job when you try to combine them.

You take the plunge. Then you face isolation. Some on the medical staff feel you have gone over to the dark side or, as Dr. Fernandez says, "feel you are a traitor". Some administrators wonder what value a physician adds to administration. In short, you face a credibility issue with both sides. Five years after taking the plunge, credibility still intact, I offer the following advice.

First, develop honest, open communication. Take to heart Dr. Fernandez's insight: "One of my most important duties is to translate and communicate others' ideas". A scheduled weekly meeting, not only with the administrative leaders but also with the medical leaders, is very helpful. We also developed a monthly meeting with senior management and the top medical leaders to improve communication and do some problem-solving. We send copies of important discussions with physicians to the chief of staff, the CEO, and the COO of our organisation.

Second, identify the formal and informal physician-leaders, and get their buy-in for any major project that you want to implement. Doing this takes patience and the ability to educate, but the long-term result is well worth the effort. With stronger support from some of the influential physician-leaders of the Clinic, perhaps Dr. Fernandez could have avoided his feelings that "by the time I have made ten decisions, I have irritated everyone". At times, you still wonder what hat you wear. Can you really do justice to both medical-staff needs and administrative needs? At times, you feel ambivalence about whether you are being objective or leaning towards one side or the other.

Another feeling that is likely to surface is frustration that you lack both the information and management skills necessary to be a successful physician-executive. We spend years in medical education before becoming physicians, and we would be mistaken to think that we can get by with less than a major educational effort in the transition to management. As Dr. Fernandez points out, excellent educational opportunities exist. The American College of Physician Executives' Institute's courses and its series of Physicians-in-Management programmes are helpful in developing operational managerial skills. The Estes Park seminars bring together physicians, board members, and administrators to hear and discuss the global issues that affect health care. Horty and Springer's seminars present the legal aspects of everything from medical-staff bylaws to joint ventures. These examples represent only a fraction of the educational opportunities available to physician-executives. The important thing to understand is that to avoid frustration and potential failure, you need an intense, ongoing educational effort.

Despite the finest educational experiences, most of the learning experience is on-the-job training and learning from your mistakes. This experiential growth in leadership skills and vision can help a physician-executive lead the organisation to its next stage of development.

How do I feel about being a physician-executive? I love it. I love the challenges of helping physicians and administrators work together to develop the clinical and administrative systems that will reshape health care in our community. I feel renewed and energised. At times I miss the direct patient contact, but for me, the plunge has been worthwhile.

I have mixed feelings about Dr. Fernandez and his experience at the Nalle Clinic. I was uncomfortable with the adversarial relationships that developed at the Clinic between the physician-CEO and the organisation. Does the physician-CEO have to feel, as Dr. Fernandez felt, like a general who must lose some of the troops to win the war?[14] I hope we can develop less war-like processes to change organisational cultures.

---

[14] See p. 115 for quotation.

I see on the horizon the principles of total quality management and trainings (such as Temenos's® *ABCs of Win-Win Relationships*), helping physician-CEOs and their organisations to deal with each other in a healthier manner.

On the other hand, I say to Dr. Fernandez, "Job well done! You facilitated the critical transition of the Nalle Clinic into a Stage-II organisation. Your articulation of your role and feelings during this transition will be of great value to the physician-executives who follow in your footsteps."

Commentary

The legal nuts and bolts of transition

Keith Korenchuk
Partner: Parker, Poe, Adams & Bernstein

WHILE THE Nalle Clinic had had a relationship with its law firm since at least 1950, the nature and level of services had been sporadic. In 1982 the Clinic, sensing a need for a more businesslike approach to its affairs, expressed a desire for a "more proactive" approach from its lawyers. I joined the firm in the fall of that year, beginning my professional relationship with the Clinic and its new Medical Director, Ray Fernandez.

As the Clinic changed from a Stage-I to a Stage-II organisation, I was a participant, not a neutral observer. Commenting on this transition, I benefit from hindsight and from my current role as a health-care attorney representing many medical groups.

Stage-I organisations, whether called by that name, or termed "medical condominiums" or "cottage industries", have a variety of common legal characteristics. First, these organisations typically employ their physicians through employment contracts that are written from the individual's perspective rather than the group's. In many ways these documents express the concept that the medical group is merely a collection of individuals whose rights are protected at the expense of the group's rights. These contracts result from physicians' desires to protect their compensation, benefits, and autonomy. The legal work is often prepared by an attorney who is a personal friend of individual physicians rather than by a law firm representing the group as a whole. Second, restrictive covenants, a mechanism whereby the group protects itself against potential competition created from within, are often nonexistent or not comprehensively drafted. Again, individual interests and autonomy are protected at the expense of the group. Third, group governance through its board of directors and a leadership team is often lacking or undeveloped. Many groups continue to operate as a pure democracy without defined leaders (ergo, anarchy), or, at the very least, a large and unworkable board which cannot make decisions on a timely basis. Thus, individual physicians in a Stage-I organisation find it difficult to think of themselves as a group. The individual and his or her practice remain an autonomous entity.

Stage-II organisations typically exhibit an entirely different set of legal characteristics. First, employment agreements favour the group—for example, in decision-making. Second, restrictive covenants are accepted and recognised as a valuable tool for protecting the goodwill of the group. These covenants are comprehensively drafted to give the group every conceivable enforcement advantage. Finally, the board of directors develops into a small group with real decision-making authority. Since issues are fully developed with appropriate recommendations before they are presented to the board, meetings run efficiently.

In the early 1980s the Nalle Clinic exhibited classic Stage-I legal symptoms, yet it was already in transition. A major revision of the Clinic's employment relationships had strengthened the Clinic's group position. In addition, the Clinic recognised the need for more pro-active leadership, placing Dr. Fernandez in the role of Medical Director. These early initiatives, which may at the time have been viewed as final solutions, clearly represent just the initial attempts at change. These efforts were complicated by internal and external factors: costly computer conversions, declining morale, loss of revenue and staff, compensation and capitalisation struggles, and competition from departed physicians and HMOs.

In 1984 and 1985 the Board and its Medical Director formulated plans during a retreat with Dr. Irv Rubin. The concept of an organisation of excellence was adopted, and Dr. Fernandez was promoted to CEO. Had the Clinic not been confronted with these internal and external factors, the transition from a medical condominium to a Stage-II organisation might have been accomplished according to plan. But because change cannot be statically implemented in a living, evolving organisation, the Clinic detoured from its charted course.

Let's look at four issues facing the Nalle Clinic and its CEO. Each one illustrates a nuts-and-bolts difficulty of effecting change from a Stage-I to a Stage-II organisation.

Issue one: operation of the Board

In the early 1980s the Board had eleven members, all physicians. The large number created inefficiencies, and many physicians had difficulty giving up their individual autonomy in favour of group decision-making. The Board met in the evenings, routinely past 10 p.m., often until midnight. The meetings were sporadic. While members were concerned with results, discussions were unfocused. Preliminary discussions, development of alternatives, and consensus building were all done during the Board meeting, not before. With such a process, efficiency was low, frustration, high. This operation was classic Stage-I behaviour.

At its retreat in 1984–85 the Board agreed to change its operating procedure from the medical-fraternity model. The size of the Board was decreased, thereby centralising authority. Meetings were moved from the evening to the morning, when minds were fresh and when the press of a full day of medical practice would require efficient thinking and decision making. Finally, lay representatives were added to provide business expertise.

These changes looked good on paper, but were difficult to implement for several reasons. First, the pace of change accelerated, making it difficult, if not impossible, for the Board to complete its agenda in its allotted two hours per month. Second, individual physician Board members had difficulty separating their personal positions from that of the Clinic as a whole. Third, lay Board members did not integrate well with the physician majority. On one hand, physicians were convinced that the lay business people did not understand that medicine was a unique business in which patients must come first. On the other hand, the business people were as firmly convinced that physicians were incapable of making sound fiscal decisions, such as reducing compensation or cutting expenses to solve the Clinic's financial problems.

While much of the framework for transformation to a Stage-II board was in place in 1985, the PhyCor transaction itself provided the crisis from which the impetus to overcome inertia evolved. Lay Board members and physician members who did not embrace the group concept resigned, resulting in a strong core leadership that became convinced that the PhyCor partnership was in the best long-term interests of the Clinic. This core group, led by Dr. Fernandez, provided the necessary guidance and encouragement to its staff members, enabling the Clinic physicians to enthusiastically adopt the PhyCor alternative.

The new Stage-II Board is composed of equal members of PhyCor and the medical group. The Board continuously confronts new challenges. Leadership, organisation, and decision-making remain critical for the Board, the Medical Director, and CEO. The painful experiences of moving from Stage I were not in vain, and the benefits of arriving at Stage II will not be lost.

Issue two: stock ownership in the clinic

For many years the physicians struggled with how the Clinic should be owned and who should vote for its Board. Historically, physicians used a percentage of their income to purchase stock each year. Stock ownership created two rights: 1) it allowed a shareholder to elect the Board of Directors; and 2) it conveyed ownership in the assets of the Nalle Clinic. However, the stock valuation method did not give the physicians the benefit of any appreciating equity in their business. Physicians viewed stock ownership as something that was required as "dues", so they gave little thought to the capital needs of the corporation. This method of operation was not unusual for smaller medical groups, which viewed themselves as collections of individuals rather than as a group.

In the 1984–85 period, a new strategy allowed the Clinic to evolve from a collection of individuals to an institution. This strategy required all physicians to own sixty shares of stock by purchasing three shares a year. Physicians who owned over sixty shares were invited to resell them to the Clinic. By requiring three shares to be purchased each year, rather than requiring a certain percentage of income to be contributed, the Clinic decided that a physician's income should not dictate his or her ultimate equity position in the company. Voting rights also changed in the direction of equality. Ultimately, everyone who had been at the Clinic for twenty years would have an equal voice in operations, regardless of speciality or income.

Again, theory was one thing and practice, another. First, some physicians refused to sell their shares, leaving several senior physicians with a large number of shares and a disproportionate control over who was elected to the Board. Second, the three-shares-per-year rule created a slow process by which physicians were deemed equals. Third, physicians grumbled about the cost to their take-home income. (There was the expense of hiring a full-time medical director/CEO. In addition, as salaries were paid according to a formula, some star performers saw their paycheques slashed.) Finally, the three shares purchased each year was not a significant amount that would improve the Clinic's ability to raise capital. Thus, the initial attempt at supporting the transition to Stage II through stock ownership fell short.

The turmoil of 1989–90 provided an opportunity to further reorient the Clinic philosophy. In order to foster group cohesiveness, share ownership and voting for the Board were separated from the control of Clinic assets. With respect to stock ownership, physicians who became senior staff physicians could immediately become shareholders on the same basis as any other Clinic shareholder. This reorganisation recognised that physicians who were granted senior staff status should have an equal vote in the governance of the group, thus becoming group members as opposed to individual shareholders. The Clinic sold much of its non-real-estate assets to PhyCor, thereby eliminating the need for shareholders to own them. In addition, the real-estate assets were removed from the Clinic itself and placed in a limited partnership composed of its physicians. This plan encouraged physicians to remain loyal to the institution. Finally, Stage-II status could be achieved by securing access to capital through the new financial partner, PhyCor.

In summary, changes begun in 1984–85 resulted in a sweeping change of the Clinic's asset and ownership strategy. Ultimately the Clinic transformed from a fraternity into an institutional-based healthcare organisation.

Issue three: restrictive covenants

In the medical-condominium model, the restrictive covenant is disfavoured because it inhibits individual mobility by protecting group viability. In the early 1980s individual physicians at the Clinic were suspicious of restrictive covenants, viewing them as an intrusion on their ability to practise medicine. While the Clinic had instituted restrictive covenants in its contracts, they were prepared in such a way as to favour the individual at the expense of the group. In addition, the physician Board members retained their individual perspective in evaluating restrictive covenants. The value of restrictive covenants in protecting the goodwill of the group was often overlooked. Often the Board was reluctant to enforce a covenant, favouring a negotiated exit arrangement that inevitably resulted in the creation of a competitor who often had received his or her start by tapping into the goodwill of the Nalle Clinic. Costs mounted as physicians departed, taking patients with them. The associated costs in recruitment, lost revenue, and lost market share created serious financial consequences. In spite of mounting concern that physician departures impaired the group, little was done to strengthen enforcement policies. The Clinic also retained its long-standing policy that physicians with ten years of service were no longer subject to the restrictive covenants.

The catalyst for Stage-II change in restrictive covenants was PhyCor. PhyCor required that all Clinic physicians, new and established, execute significantly more comprehensive agreements. Business considerations dictated that stronger enforcement practices now be implemented. The covenants limited individual freedom to practice in exchange for a benefit in strengthening the organisation. The Board and its Medical Director recognised that restrictive covenants had a significant role in making divorce a less easily taken route in resolving disputes. It is clear that, with PhyCor's assistance and in light of the experience with no-fault divorce in the late 1980s, the medical group achieved a Stage-II view of the role of a restrictive covenant.

Issue four: role of the CEO

As discussed previously, the Nalle Clinic had difficulty defining the role for its physician-CEO. Like many patients, the Clinic found it difficult to define for its caregiver where it hurt, so the CEO was constantly evaluating his patient. He wore different hats with different groups. To the Stage-I Board, the CEO often played an implementing role, waiting for instructions before acting. This role slowly evolved to a leadership position. To individual physicians the CEO was a communicator and a lightning rod for frustrations. To consultants the CEO was the healer and advocate, conscious of what was needed by his patient, the Clinic.

In treating his patient in 1989, Dr. Fernandez recognised that both internal and external factors were impeding the transition to Stage II (though he might not have called it that), and he became convinced that the most viable strategy was to implement the PhyCor relationship and to make sure it succeeded, even though that success meant a change in his own role as CEO. However, in my view, this process was not at all like Dr. Fernandez's statement that "the patient was referred to a specialist". Clearly, without his own leadership in the evaluation, analysis, and implementation of the PhyCor agreement, the Clinic's evolution to Stage II would not have occurred so quickly. One who was so in touch with his patient and who was continuously involved in hands-on care was the real "specialist". The CEO was able to conclude that PhyCor represented a vehicle for achieving organisational change. While the Medical Director-CEO became Medical Director in the process, the strategy helped his patient through a temporary illness, and led to a group-practice transformation.

Conclusion

To survive and prosper, medical groups must confront the transition from a bunch of individuals to a cohesive group. This change is not a total transformation; it is a shift in the balance of power. Each group must require its individuals to trust the group more, to surrender their individual rights for the common good, and to subscribe to the group mission. Different individual interests will always create tension in organisations, so effecting change inevitably creates adversarial relationships. Those who propose change must be prepared for resistance from those who do not want to change. The challenge for medical-practice leaders, one successfully faced by Dr. Fernandez, is to channel that change, to evaluate the patient, and to implement strategies that work. Groups which make this transition have bright futures. As this case study of the Nalle Clinic has shown, successful implementation may require a variety of strategies, some of which can only be discerned after the process is well under way. The ability to understand and implement the necessary legal transformation to Stage-II behaviour is vital to a leader's fulfilment of his duty to his patient.

Commentary

The patient speaks

John L. Benedum, MD
President of the Nalle Clinic Board of Directors

Editor's note: While we have entitled this brief commentary "The Patient Speaks",
it would be inappropriate and unfair to presume that any single individual can
speak for the entire Nalle Clinic. Many years together in the trenches have brought
Dr. Fernandez and Dr. Benedum to a treasured level of mutual trust and respect.
While some of Dr. Benedum's observations from the patient's perspective might be
seen by others as critical, they are offered and received as gifts of genuine caring.
Such is the power of win-win relationships among valued friends and colleagues,
among providers and patients. Without honest, direct, heart-to-heart feedback,
there can be little learning, growth, development, and healing.

THIS PATIENT-ORGANISATION is well known to me. I joined the
Nalle Clinic in 1979 as one of the first two general internists
added to the group. Two years later I was elected to the governing Board of Directors. I had a keen interest in guiding the direction of
the Clinic and represented a primary-care constituency. Through the
years described in the Case Report, I was an active observer and participant in those changes. I would like to share my perspective on the
Clinic and the career of my colleague, friend, and attending physician,
Ray Fernandez.

The Nalle Clinic was Charlotte's only significant health-care group,
outside of the hospitals, in the early 1980's. We invested a great deal of
energy, time, and money to restructuring our decision-making processes
and administrative roles. I recall considerable scepticism and resistance
from many members of the group. Organisational psychology and management terminology were foreign to most of us on the Board of

Directors. Admittedly, we were much less comfortable in these roles compared to our more traditional physician roles. For example, it was a monumental effort to achieve consensus on the mission of this developing organisation!

We spent so much time reorganising and positioning ourselves for a future that we thought was going to be more competitive and more demanding that we failed to nurture and accommodate some factions within the group. The Clinic's leadership decided that the interests of the whole organisation came first. Unable to see the future benefits of this investment in a growing organisation, some physicians and departments left the Clinic. Their retreat to simpler, single-speciality practices compounded our financial stresses and undermined our spirit.

The decision to hire a part-time Medical Director from within the ranks of the Clinic, someone we all knew and trusted, speaks to the caution with which we were testing these new waters. The Board had a list of chores that they thought would be best done by a physician: being a liaison between physicians and administration, recruiting new staff and negotiating their contracts, and co-ordinating physician committees. The role of the Medical Director and then the Medical Director/CEO developed around Dr. Fernandez, his personality and skills.

In the care of a patient with an identified illness, there are standards of care and an accepted treatment plan. In a changing medical environment, the course that our medical group should take was not clear to any of us. We assigned a formidable task to our physician colleague. He agreed to trade quick feedback and appreciation from his patient interactions (his patients miss him yet today), for an often hostile environment where gratification is, at best, delayed or often non-existent.

As we all became more comfortable thinking of the organisation as having a life of its own, it became easier to delineate responsibilities and authority to administrative team members. By virtue of his devotion, energies, and communication skills, Dr. Fernandez became the natural leader in this transition period. He had his critics, for sure, but with patience and persuasion he guided the organisation towards a more efficient structure. Physicians and the Board gradually seemed more willing to relinquish some of their individual control in the best interests of the group. There was never a ground swell of unanimous support. Some physicians stated emphatically that this was not the Clinic that they had joined and that they could no longer live with this new direction and its influences on their autonomy and style of practice.

Slowly and cautiously, changes occurred. We were still unwilling to make dramatic changes in personnel and business practices. Dr. Fernandez, the officers and the Board of Directors shared responsibility for decisions leading to the increasing financial problems. In retrospect, however, I wonder if our organisation would have survived the challenges of 1988–89 had we not restructured. Even at that point, many of us were still clinging to the idea that the situation would improve and things would work out. They always had in the past! To chart our course and move confidently into an uncertain future, we kept searching for more data, better data, more inspirational leadership, and more expert analysis. If we could only find that visionary who possessed all the other executive qualities, surely we could weather this storm. We began to search for a more experienced, hard-nosed, detail-oriented administrator to complement Dr. Fernandez's visionary, soft style. My interpretation of the feelings of several Board members and physicians was that, although Dr. Fernandez was appreciated for his ability to listen and to resolve conflicts, he was not capable of critically analysing the financial data. I think that he did not get creative solutions or adequate analysis from his administrative staff and was unwilling to change that management team significantly. As our back-office operations and systems were obviously unsuccessful, we had an even greater need of a strong-handed turnaround expert.

It seems clear to me now that this problem developed over several years. We hire, train, and reward administrators to be subservient to the physician-run corporation. Then we criticise them when they speak their own mind. At the same time, we physicians are going along with our day-to-day routine and busy practices, assuming that someone is minding the store ... until something upsets our personal worlds. I don't think the physician Board members or the administration stayed abreast of our financial situation. When the crisis flared up, Dr. Fernandez took most of the heat. Perhaps this was appropriate. To his credit, he remained poised and professional. He did not panic when his patient was haemorrhaging.

The organisation was slowly maturing, but we felt a sense of urgency in the summer of 1989. Rather than dismiss Dr. Fernandez, as some urged, we agreed to search for a saviour. The death of the Nalle Clinic as a multi-speciality group was considered only as a last resort. We looked locally and we hired a search firm. Those unsuccessful efforts and our lack of confidence in our own abilities to turn the business around fuelled our search for a corporate partner. I suggested looking outside the medical field because I thought that such business expertise did not exist in traditional clinic settings.

To Dr. Fernandez's credit, he initiated and participated in a search for a partner who could provide the necessary capital and business expertise. With PhyCor came a renewed hope, energy, and a recovery of our confidence in the Clinic: with the new personnel and capital, we would be able to achieve our goals.

A marketing consultant's perspective

Bruce Fritch

President of Fritch Consulting, Charlotte, North Carolina

T HE PHYSICIANS at the Nalle Clinic were bright, earnest physicians, successful and proud in their individual practices. Why did they experience so much difficulty and turmoil when facing the challenges of a mutual purpose? What can we learn from this extraordinary case study that can help us avoid its pitfalls? Is it reasonable to work towards the quality patient-care standards of Japan's St. Marguerite Hospital and still hope to achieve attractive profitability goals?

Preview

In this commentary I will relate the case of the Nalle Clinic and perhaps Every Clinic to factors which are contributing to the persistence of dysfunctional Stage-I phenomena. I will point to the importance of power in relationships and to our responsibility for shaping the quality of relationships. For it isn't enough to understand the characteristics of Stages I, II, and III. We must learn to build transition bridges from one to the other.

It is possible to build a profitable, quality-oriented group practice with a strategy that encompasses profit as well as standards of medical competence and patient care. Shaping such an organisation begins with the personal influence of the chief executive officer *and* the board of directors, department managers, and professional and lay staffs. The whole organisation must have several ingredients: a mutual purpose, an acceptance of their intense interdependence, and the will and the skill to resolve the inevitable conflicts and frustrations that arise. Most important, it must take action. Initially what we as individual practitioners can do is increase our interpersonal skills and awareness, our effectiveness as *leaders*. We must strengthen the quality of our relationships within the marketplace (with patients and referring physicians), and within our professional organisations today.

The phenomena of power and influence

Let's begin by looking at John French and Bertram Raven's[15] widely regarded model describing five common bases of power: reward, coercive, referent, legitimate, and expert. Of these, legitimate and expert are most relevant here.

Legitimate power is based on people's belief that *agents* of authority (for example, government or a CEO), have a legitimate right to prescribe behaviour for them. Legitimate power stems from values we internalised growing up. It manifests in our belief that someone or some group has the "legitimate right to influence" a person, and that that person has an "*obligation* [italics added] to accept this influence".[16] While factors such as age, intelligence, and physical characteristics may influence legitimate power, it is often bestowed on someone by an empowering licensing agency. For example, the AMA, state medical boards, and medical schools are legitimising agencies of authority. With legitimate power, the extent of the authority is generally specified when the power is designated (for example, the conferring of Board Certification). If actions extend outside this authority, explicit resistance and a decrease in power is likely (as we have seen when schools boards attempted to censor classroom books).

Expert power originates from having superior knowledge or ability in specific areas. The strength of expert power "varies with the extent of knowledge or perception" of knowledge which a person attributes to the agent of authority.[17] Several requirements are at work:

1. Others must have confidence that the expert has knowledge.
2. Expert power is restricted to a given field of expertise. Although there may be a halo effect (evidenced by the number of star athletes who

---

[15] "The Bases of Social Power", in *Group Dynamics: Research and Theory*, 3rd ed., ed by Dorwin Cartwright and Alvin Zander, (New York: Harper & Row, 1968), pp. 262–268. Originally published in *Studies in Social Power*, D. Cartwright, ed. (Ann Arbor, Mich.: Institute for Social Research, 1959).
[16] *Ibid.* p. 265.
[17] *Ibid.* p. 267.

promote breakfast cereals or underwear), most expert power is limited. When others conclude that the expert is out of line, "an undermining of confidence seems to take place".[18]

3. Others must perceive that the expert is trustworthy—credible and reliable. Trust builds over time by doing the little things right all of the time. If the little things are neglected, a negative halo effect can occur. For example, airlines that don't clean coffee stains from tray tables can contribute to a moment of passenger anxiety about the quality of engine maintenance. Similarly, physicians who can't keep their appointment-time promises contribute to the discontent (disease) of their patients.

What's happening to the regard for authority?

Authority is most simply defined as "the ability to get a desired response to one's wishes". No desired response, no authority. Hence, authority is power of the most practical sort, influencing demand for services and professional relationships alike. In the past we *automatically* depended on our experts. But the fundamental nature of how people relate to authority has changed.

Since World War II, Americans have become sceptical, even cynical, of authority. Many events have contributed to the change, including Watergate, computerised trading scandals, hazardous waste accumulation, and exposure of inept public officials and immoral evangelists. The change is reflected in the civil rights movement, contraception, feminism, government watchdog committees, and voter apathy.

Not until the Vietnam War did attitudes begin to shift on a large scale, considerably fostered and conveyed by the news media. Americans questioned the morality of being in Vietnam; the competence of military and political leaders to wage an effective war; and the ethics and honesty of the media, the military, and the government. The effect was protests and marches, rocks and tear gas. There was a tremendous polarisation in regard for traditional authority.

Other factors amplified the change in public regard for authority: the news media (performing as news makers, rather than news reporters); microcomputers and other high-tech, intelligence-enhancing tools (placing the power of information and technology into the hands of the many); and terrorism and the assassinations of President Kennedy,

---

[18] *Ibid.* p. 268.

Bobby Kennedy, and Martin Luther King, Jr. (weakening the public's faith in authorities' ability to protect and defend).

Scepticism grew in the 1980s. Changes in public regard for authority exploded world-wide. From brave efforts by Polish shipyard workers to the bitter response to political and social incompetence in Rumania, to Soviet *Glasnost*, to resisting apartheid in South Africa, people are insisting on new relationships with authorities and are setting aside those which are fundamentally unequal or disrespectful.

I think the changes in the public's regard for authority, with the commensurate demand for relationships of greater quality, is the most significant factor influencing the effectiveness of professional organisations today. I have seen its growth in the health-care marketplace since the mid-1980s. And it is evolving in other professional services markets, such as accounting and management consulting. Now the impact on health-care organisations is particularly dramatic.

A perspective for viewing: a new consumerism

Over the past decade a new consumerism has been evolving, aimed at relationships in the professions. It is based on scepticism about professionals and an unwillingness to tolerate behaviour, intentional or not, that diminishes the consumer's self-esteem. New-consumer patients want to be treated as persons, not just as a body of symptoms. The appearance of a white coat does not convey carte-blanche authority. They challenge the medical experts' diagnoses, fees, and range of authority.

The sports and fitness movement has been especially pivotal in shaping a new view of physicians. Millions of tennis, running, and exercise buffs began reading about exercise, nutrition, and fitness. Visiting their physicians, they seized the opportunity to verify the tips they had acquired. Too many discovered that their physicians' knowledge of wellness was inadequate. This perception was amplified if these doctors smoked or were overweight, and did not practice what they preached. As a result, scepticism and doubt encroached on these patients' traditionally compliant attitudes.

The self-help movement further eroded the dependence on physician authority. As people learned to take greater responsibility for their own well-being, they came face to face with the humanness of their healers. Patients, such as Norman Cousins, who wrote *Anatomy of an Illness*, discovered that they could contribute to their own health as much as, or more than, physicians.

The new consumerism entails a change in the relationship with authorities, both legitimate and expert. The confidence and trustworthiness necessary for expert power must be regained through a team relationship. Today, if patients don't experience the relationship or medical quality they expect, they are likely to seek help elsewhere.

Power dynamics in physician-patient relationships

With the expert power of miracle drugs and space-age technology at their disposal, doctors have been accused of having a superior attitude, a priestly mien. Sometimes this is characterised by the lack of information that physicians communicate to patients. Lack of communication, whether from physician to patient or to referring physician, can be interpreted as deceitful. Patients conclude that too often there is a lack of respect: physician as priest, patient as child.

Curiously, physicians tell me they rarely see it this way. "Respect patients? Of course I respect my patients!"—as though the suggestion were absurd. Juggling new technologies, competitive pressures, and third-party payment guidelines, physicians are called on to accept one more challenge, that of assertive, unsolicitous patients.

Patients, especially those over 55 years old, have done their part to maintain the priestly mien by behaving subserviently with their doctors. They didn't question why their doctors did not meet their needs for information and availability.

Recently a 71-year-old woman, complaining of sore legs and excessive fatigue, visited her doctor. Sitting in an examination room, her resting pulse was 143. The physician ordered her into the hospital where she was extensively tested for three days and nights, treated according to findings, and released on drug therapy. Her children—ages 32, 43, and 45, who lived out of state—persistently inquired about her condition. The woman, all the while pleased with her physician, could never offer an informed response. She had not been told, and she was reluctant to inquire for information that the doctor had not volunteered. If the doctor had wanted her to know, she thought, he would have told her.

Who was right? Her adult children were infuriated, vowing never to let a physician get away with such disrespect and so-called treatment. To them, the quality of the physician's relationship with their mother was inappropriate. Some readers will argue that if the physician had offered treatment and met the patient's expectations, then the physician acted appropriately. Another issue, however, is how future patients (e.g., the three adult children), will respond to the same treatment. *What is the right thing for the physician to do?* The quality of the relationship is of growing importance in the marketplace.

However, we must not lose sight of the point that market share is a result. The purpose of improving the relationship is improving the quality of care. In spirit, the new consumerism is reminding the profession of the Hippocratic Oath: "In every house where I come, I will enter only for the good of my patients".

It is a massive overstatement that physicians have a genetic, personality-driven, or med-school-instilled propensity to be uninformative, unavailable, and unresponsive. Regardless of the reason, many of us recognise that another dynamic is operating. The malpractice mania and doctor bashing we are seeing is being caused, psychologically, by a sense that a fiduciary trust has been broken. Isn't it curious that my old family doctor knew less and had less technology than today's experts, yet we trusted him implicitly? Why would it never have occurred to my parents to sue him even if he made a lethal mistake? This is the kind of issue that I believe needs more careful attention.

MDs are not, in my view, sole causal agents. Like all of us, they are caught in a living dynamic transformation. The change in how people relate to authority is purging the priestly mien from physicians' choices of acceptable attitudes. This change makes it impossible, as well as undesirable, for physicians to focus only on the quality of their technology and their competence at their craft, devoting little effort or awareness to the quality of their professional relationships. Because of the significance of their roles in society, we look to physicians to embrace a leadership challenge: to first heal themselves.

Recommendations for symptoms of ineffective patient relationships

Trust is essential in a physician-patient relationship. Because of circumstances of illness, one party is more helpless than the other party. The unique challenge to many professional relationships is that the situation puts one party in a one-down position. This challenges the helper to (a) accept the other's helplessness as being real while (b) still treating the other as a full person. And it is the helper's professional responsibility (fiduciary trust) to take the initiative and to be helpful. Here, help is evaluated from the perspective of the party being helped. The challenge is great. Who among us finds it easy to be informative, available, and responsive to a person who, in his or her position as patient, represents a potential malpractice threat or production inefficiency?

To heal the relationships, physicians must consciously demonstrate their care and compassion for each patient. New-consumer patients want their physicians to be team-mates, partners in health. As we will see in the next sections, collaborative teamwork can become the theme of the authority relationships in the 1990s.

Power dynamics in physician-group relationships

Physicians' relationships with legitimate power (represented to the physicians within their organisations by the CEO, the board, and the administration) have been changing, too. Reflecting a new consumerism of their own, physicians also express, and react to, legitimate and expert power in very significant ways. In particular, physicians are less willing to let others govern the organisation without receiving information and assurances from those in charge. Changes in the relationship that physicians experience within their own organisational environment parallel the changes discussed here in physician-patient relationships. The point is, the shift in regard for authority applies equally.

Summary of the Nalle Clinic situation in the 1980s

Bursting with Stage-I energy, the Nalle Clinic was the quintessential fraternity model. Yet fraternal it was not. Despite the efficient and professional conduct of physicians in their individual practices, the collective team of physicians did not work together effectively. Forces of the self-centred traits typical of a Stage-I organisation were stronger than the attractions of mutual purpose and high-quality teamwork. Driving these Stage-I behaviours was the physician at odds with the Clinic's legitimate authority: the Board and especially the CEO (legitimate power personified).

Lacking confidence in management's expertise, the physician group frustrated *itself* with the lack of decision making progress. Administrative and Board-level decisions were delayed until the assembled all-physician staff (nearly 80!) could debate and determine the course of action (about one meeting per month). Predictably, personal agendas intruded on organisational purposes; divisiveness stamped out interdependence. Executive appropriateness was based more on conformity with the wishes of the all-physician staff than on accepted standards of management. In particular, appropriateness was rarely based on the decision of those nominally responsible for decision making (i.e., the CEO, Board, and administrators). Second-guessing by the all-physician staff resulted in paralysis in daily administrative and operational decision making. This paralysis spread to the Board of Directors, inhibiting their ability to deal with policy issues.

A lack of interpersonal skills and a lack of organisational effectiveness in such Stage-I groups is understandable. What medical school emphasises relationship philosophy and skills? Physicians' training focuses on knowledge, tools, and craft—on the hard sciences of medicine and not on the softer, interpersonal arts of healing. What is the root cause of physician behaviour that others experience as abusive to self-esteem? Recent research has put it at the hands and feet of physicians' teachers.[19] In other words, physicians are just practising what they learned. It is the managers and executives in non-medical business organisations who receive extensive human-development training.[20] It is only the most enlightened of physicians and physician-executives who create time in their busy schedules for interpersonal skill-building training. For health-care organisations moving into the 21st century this, *too*, must change.

Recommendations for treating symptoms of organisational ineffectiveness

Step 1. Administrators and physicians must learn to appreciate and respect their differences. One group has a heart-felt understanding of the operation of a business; and the other, of the business of operations. They need each other to achieve their heart-felt mutual purpose: providing quality care.

Step 2. Physicians, as leaders, must develop their interpersonal skills. On-the-job learning will be necessary. When physicians and administrators attend seminars together on management and systems of monitoring quality care, they report, "We now understand each other better".

Step 3. Physicians must demonstrate greater respect and a willingness to learn from others. The physician staff at Every Clinic must attempt to understand and implement the recommendations of their committees

---

[19] Henry K. Silver, MD and Anita Duhl Glicken, MSW, "Medical Student Abuse: Incidence, Severity, and Significance", *JAMA*, 263, no. 4, (26 January 1990), pp. 527–537.
[20] For a discussion of the link between quality improvement and behaviour towards customers, see Irwin Rubin and Robert Inguagiato, "Behavioral Quality Assurance: A Transforming Experience", *Physician Executive*, 16, no. 5, (Sept.–Oct. 1990), pp. 30–33.

who have done careful research. In the same spirit, administrators must respect physicians' ability and desire to learn about management and organisational leadership.

These philosophies, skills, and perspectives all transfer to relationships with patients and referring physicians. As a direct consequence, they will affect the bottom line. Yes, we can have the quality patient care of Japan's St. Marguerite along with business prosperity. The physician group that is willing to strive towards a mutual purpose, work as a team, and abide by high-performance team agreements can bridge to Stage II.

The action steps to recovery

Knowledge about what needs improvement is not a mystery to any doctor, lawyer, or chief executive. The steps to recovery are specific:

1. Admit that what we have is not good enough, not working well enough, yet.
2. Stop doing what we've done in the past that we know is not helping.
3. Decide together with colleagues what has to be done. We will have to learn how to do some of the things we know we need to do, and we will need to practise daily, preferably together.

As long as we allow ourselves to be distracted from our mutual primary purpose, our dependent patients have no choice but to continue to struggle to get our attention with any means at their disposal. Until we learn to work together as a quality team, we have no right to expect any more from our patients.

Our regard for authority has been changing. We can expect it to evolve into this decade and beyond. Responding sufficiently in the areas of human relations and team building will be physicians'—professionals'—performance challenge of the 1990s and beyond.

Commentary

Turbulent passages of change and the dynamics of power

Irwin Rubin, PhD

Who is the speaker here, and who is being accused?

> "You don't fully explain the reasons for your decisions."
> "You use jargon instead of simple language I can understand."
> "You're difficult to reach by phone."
> "You're hard to get an appointment with."
> "You treat me like a little child, not an adult."
> "You're more concerned about money than about quality care."

The most common response is "patients are accusing their physician providers". Surprise! There is another correct answer: "physicians are accusing their managerial providers". The motivation behind both sets of accusations is improvement in the quality of care. Yet allies are acting like enemies.

Power, and its redistribution and rebalancing, create strong emotional reactions. Many years ago I was working with a health-care organisation that used an interdisciplinary team approach. Team-leader physicians resisted our team-building project because they feared that their power was about to be usurped. As one physician put it, "I don't have time or need for this touchy-feely stuff!" At the end of the project, he said with relief, "I still make 75% of the decisions on this team ... but now I do it after consulting with my team-mates!"

Reducing physicians' power—that is, reducing their responsibility for medical decisions—is not the objective. Expanding their power base, increasing their total sphere of influence, is one challenge. The second is to reframe our negative reaction to the word *power*. As we have seen in Bruce Fritch's commentary, deep forces in society have changed patients' relationship with expert power. No longer is the patient willing to passively swallow all the pills the physician prescribes. Psychologically, the current malpractice mania can be seen as the necessary, although painful and dysfunctional, counterdependent phase preceding a more adult-to-adult relationship.

Physicians are the common denominator in both answers to the flying accusations beginning this commentary. In one case, physicians are on the pointy end of the arrow; in the other, they are on the feather end. Adding TLC, the healing power of their whole persons, along with sophisticated intellects and technology will have two effects for physicians: (1) increasing the quality of care, and (2) developing both empathy and a win-win approach towards their managerial leadership. The healthier the organisation, the greater the quality of care that patients receive. In other words, the change in the relationship we see as being necessary between MDs and their patients will mirror the changes we see needing to occur in the relationship between physicians and administrators. This is one of the leadership challenges in health care, and physicians are the key.

Physicians as individuals, as dependent members of health-care organisations, express their changing regard for the authority of their providers in governance issues. The case of the Nalle Clinic demonstrates a power struggle taking place in many Stage-I fraternity organisations: physicians are less willing to let others govern the organisation (make priestly pronouncements), without being informed. Their Stage-I level of maturity results in ambivalence, as Dr. Fernandez has noted:

> Although all physicians demanded "better management", their disdain for bureaucracy and administration intensified. Physicians did not volunteer to serve on the Board of Directors. Rather, like Monday morning quarterbacks, many knew exactly what plays should have been called. Few seemed willing to leave their seats on the 50-yard line and join the battle on the astro-turf.[21]

---

[21] See p. 2.

We are not saying that teamwork has been totally absent from the relationship between physicians and their patients or between physicians and their managerial providers. Different kinds of teams are needed at various stages of development.[22] Power varies accordingly.

The balance of power shifts dramatically as organisations move from the Stage-I baseball team to the Stage-II football team to the Stage-III basketball team. Consider planning meetings. Meetings are a key forum for power plays; they're an arena where influence takes place. Specific rules prescribe how many people are allowed to meet on the pitcher's mound and how often. (Never 80 once a month!) A representative from the dugout, the head office, is only allowed one visit to these meetings before the pitcher's head must roll. When the team's on the field, other important communications (attempts at influence) must be yelled across the field or transmitted via coded body English.

By contrast, typically, no formal move is planned on a football team without a huddle of all the relevant team members. Shuttle diplomacy may operate as the coach sends in plays, but the entire team hears the word at the same time and has a chance to respond. ("I think I can beat him long with a 32X left!") The most respected and experienced quarterbacks are granted the legitimate power to use their expertise unilaterally (not autocratically), call an audible and change the play on the line of scrimmage.

As we have noted, basketball only works like magic when the meeting of the minds takes place "intuitively" or can be directed by one player while the game is being played. A basketball team, like a Stage-III organisation, is less dependent on the power of supervision and more dependent on the power of Super Vision.

It is not enough to simply understand the characteristics of various stages of development as static steady states. We must also learn how to survive and grow together during the inevitably unsteady transitions between stages. Regardless of the context (parent and child, physician and patient, professional and employing organisation), growing up is always associated with a shift in the balance of power. Learning to manage these dynamics begins with accepting some simple, though painful, truths about power and the process of change.

A counterbalancing of forces characterises an organisation in the steady state of existence, regardless of its particular stage of development. The forces pushing for change are met by virtually equal and

---

[22] See p. 53 for a discussion of the support that team members require to make the behavioural changes during major transitions, to learn how to play different games.

opposite forces of resistance, which create an equilibrium. For example, younger employees interested in growth will support new capital expansion proposals ("Our future lies in growth"), while old-timers will resist ("I'm getting ready to retire. Don't burden me with any more debt load").

This process dynamic can be subtle. In deciding to elect a physician to a management position as medical director and asking him "to devote 50% of his time to administrative matters at a salary of 50% of the average physician's income", the Nalle Clinic added to the forces of change. The idea, as Dr. Fernandez noted, "was to financially motivate the medical director to improve the physicians' incomes". On the other hand, the Board created an equal and opposing force of resistance because it "did not spell out the position's power and authority [did not give Dr. Fernandez legitimate power], except to point out that the medical director would attend Board meetings in an advisory capacity but *would not vote*" [emphasis added]. The same passive-resistant dynamic operated when Dr. Fernandez was made full-time CEO, a potentially powerful position for change. He did not ask for a formal set of performance expectations, and the Board did not offer one. Neither he nor the Board would be able to know if he was making it or not.

So the stage was set for ambiguity and its by-product, fear. Imagine how the crews of the Niña, the Pinta, and the Santa Maria felt as they sailed through uncharted seas. Their CEO promised a brave new world, but the sailors believed they were doomed to fall off a flat earth!

Successful change rests upon reducing fear and resistance. Reducing, not eliminating. Change for change's sake can be as irresponsible as resistance for resistance's sake. I believe that change strategies that focus exclusively on the power of increasing pressure will have high human costs. Logical explanations and data-driven analyses to justify needed changes are necessary but insufficient. Emotional support, TLC, is necessary to reduce this fear. For example, the fact that my physician had performed a particular surgical procedure successfully a thousand times made my head happy, but did little to soothe my gut. I had the fleeting thought that he was probably due for a failure! The fact that the professionally trained physician-managers and administrators have performed particular organisational procedures successfully in the past does little to reduce physicians' fears about who's running the store.

More than they can admit, physicians today are gripped by fear and anxiety. They are dependent on the system of an organisation, a collective, to provide the context, resources, and protection to allow them to do the job they trained for: caring for individual patients. They spend countless hours worrying about their salaries, just as patients and insurance companies complain about rising costs. They grumble about decisions made for them by others on high, just as patients resent long waiting times and prescriptions written without sufficient explanation. In part because they have not dealt with their own fears and anxieties, "many physicians are unaware that patients experience 'massive amounts of anxiety' during sickness and treatment".[23] This lack of awareness results in behaviours that patients think are insensitive. For example, probing the body with a cold instrument without explaining why, in terms they understand, can lead patients to conclude that their physician doesn't care. (Forcing budgets down physicians' throats causes gagging, too!) Less physically intrusive, but no less insensitive, is the feeling many patients get that "their time is worth nothing". They wait long periods for short visits that result in huge bills.

Respect for clients can come from surprising sources. For example, a tyre dealership in Hawaii provides quality care to its customers. If customers are forced to wait twenty minutes longer than the scheduled appointment time, they receive a cash discount.

I recently visited my doctor for a follow-up appointment. I was asked the same history questions ("Any history of heart trouble in your family? ..."), that I had answered three times the previous month. It was only when I objected that this waste of my time stopped ... but not before my trust eroded another tick.

A violated trust triggers a counterdependent reaction. In the medical profession this takes the form of malpractice mania. As medical researchers have documented,[24] factors often labelled as "the soft psychological stuff"—awareness, trust, and sensitivity—can directly impact the healing process.

Many years ago I observed physicians prescribing medication to Hispanic people living in the squalor of New York's South Bronx. These young, white, upper-class doctors said, "Take three times daily with regular meals". The look on these patients' faces seemed to say, "Yeah, as if I could afford to eat three times a day! Who are these guys in white coats? What do they know?" I saw several people drop their pills into the trash on their way out. To these patients, the doctors had no expert power. Medical research shows that 50–60% noncompliance is not uncommon.[25]

[23] Irwin Press, "The Predisposition to File Claims: The Patient's Perspective", *Law, Medicine & Health Care*, April, 1984, p. 54.
[24] *Ibid.*, pp. 53–62.
[25] *Ibid.*, p. 54.

Comparable figures are not available vis-à-vis physicians-as-patients in response to managerial directives. As Dr. Fernandez noted in his Medical Record, however, "Members of the Clinic frequently appealed the decisions made by the Board and committees. Lengthy delays in making and implementing decisions became common. The Clinic never did implement certain decisions. Over a five-year period, two separate committees studied cost accounting, but the Clinic's members would not accept any of their proposals".[26]

High tech, be it sophisticated management information systems or MRIs (Magnetic Resonance Imaging), does little to reduce people's gut fear of change. Such high tech can actually increase fear. Regardless of how carefully experts explain their MRI, only the expert really knows how—or if—it works. What can reduce resistance and fear to manageable proportions? TLC. High touch. Higher touch means changing the nature and the quality of the *relationship* between physician and patients and between physicians and administrators. Dr. Fernandez anticipated this when he noted, "One of my most important duties is to translate and communicate others' ideas", to keep people in touch. He quickly added, "However, listeners tend to mistrust a translator they must depend on".[27]

Just as a lay person can not expect to become a medical expert by reading *Reader's Digest*, physicians can ill afford to short-change the business of management by acting as if it were a profession that any bright, educated, earnest individual could learn overnight. Board meetings can no more be crammed into overscheduled patient hours than can complicated surgical procedures.

As educated consumers, we can ask good questions of our providers. *If* they take place in the context of a relationship based on mutual respect and trust, as opposed to attack and defensiveness, these questions can guide the efforts of our providers. Similarly, educated physicians can be supporters of their managerial providers if the same relationship of mutual respect and trust can be built.

Over a period of several years, a forward-thinking physician-CEO invited several hundred of his key physicians to attend a one-week, in-house seminar on management. Lay administrators were invited, too. It was a huge time investment. (You readers can tally the lost billable hours.) A personal invitation from the CEO was not easy to refuse, so many attended ... with mixed feelings. Virtually everyone finished the

---

[26] See p. 3.
[27] See p. 59.

seminar with a deeper appreciation for, and understanding of, the managerial role in the provision of quality care.

Instead of MDs approaching their organisation's managers like frightened, angry children fighting with their parents, they need to be helped to join with their colleagues in the creation of a team relationship. Physician-CEOs who can facilitate this shifting of collective power, this rebalancing, will be influencing the quality of the relationship between physicians (professionals) and their provider organisation. As this relationship grows, so will the quality of the relationship between these providers and the individual patients they serve.

As this change begins to take place, patients will find it easier to say to physicians, "With all due respect, Doctor, when you poke me with that cold instrument without telling me what you are doing, I don't feel good about it". Growing up means increasing overall quality because bedside manner is not purely a matter of marketing or PR; it is an aspect of the process of healing, which is the purpose for the relationship in the first place. Actively seeking and remaining open to, and accepting of, such feedback isn't easy when the profession and its patients have together created an ethos that attributes godliness to human beings who have earned the legitimate title of medical expert.

Physician-executives have a unique contribution to make. They have been members of the fraternity. They can empathise with the pain of slung arrows. People such as Ray Fernandez understand the dynamics of patient-provider anxiety and dependence. They know it in their heart and soul. As they earn the legitimate expertise of educated professional managers, they will be in a position to help build the bridges of transition essential to their organisation's growing up.

The bridges I see as necessary will take the form of building new interpersonal relationships. I believe that all communication is an attempt at social influence. A picture of these new, synergistic relationships can be developed using the template of the *push* and *pull* styles of communication introduced earlier.[28] Power and influence as dynamic processes, messages, take place or are carried out through communications.

The content of an expert's push behaviours would be primarily *descriptive* and *prescriptive*: "I suggest you take this medication twice daily for two weeks because you have symptoms A, B, and C, and this drug is highly effective in these cases". "You need to extend office hours into the evening and weekends because our patient satisfaction surveys show this as a priority need". If experts with a priestly mien believe that

---

[28] See p. 50.

it is their divine right to pontificate without explanation, prescriptions offered without clear, detailed, descriptive reasons or explanations will likely result.

An expert's *pull* behaviours would be narrowly confined to *attending* (listening) and *asking*. The *asking* would be very specific, for example, "Do you have any questions about my prescription?" "Have you completed your department's five-year plan yet?" Here again, if an expert's ego has gotten out of hand, impatience creeps in, and *attending* behaviours get cut short.

A team, adult-to-adult relationship does not eliminate the above, but rather expands it in terms of styles of behaviour. The expert enthusiastically and openly *asks* for suggestions: "What do you think is causing the problem? How have you considered changing the situation?" Since the patient would have an equal role in the relationship, the physician would exhibit more *understanding* behaviours: (a) to the patient "So what you're telling me is, you tend to skip breakfast and lunch regularly", and (b) to a colleague: "Our disagreement seems to stem from my needing to have 24-hour coverage and your not wanting to take any night call". Of course, true teamwork is impossible without mutual respect and empathy.

Comparable changes would be seen on the *push* side. The patient (or employee) and the expert (physician or manager) would both be offering prescriptions, suggestions, to improve the situation. Explanations of descriptive facts and reasons would be detailed, in language the *receiver* could understand, and would be offered willingly, not grudgingly. An educated, knowledgeable patient or employee is a valuable asset.

Such rebalancing, realignment, and reattunement will be very difficult for people intent on sailing in the narrow channels of expert power. I emphasise that each party has the power to be 100% responsible for their part in the relationship. If patients change their behaviour with their doctors, then the relationship with their doctors will be different. If the doctors are more informative with their patients, then their relationship with their patients will be different. When the Nalle Clinic began to change its relationship with its physician-staff, some left because they liked the old way better.

There is a price to these changes: vulnerability. Dr. Berman said it well:

> Acknowledging their expertise and your own deficiencies and asking for their help are critical and are not—as might be initially feared—at all inconsistent with the authoritative style recommended earlier. Confidence and strength are required to know and own one's

limitations. Since people expect physicians to be egotists, a bit of honest humility goes a long way—especially when the truth of such an attitude is so apparent.[29]

Bluffing, a *push* behaviour motivated by fear, gets interpreted as arrogance; and it increases others' resistance. Acknowledging our own deficiencies reduces our own and others' fears, clearing the path for change. As the old adage goes, the truth sets us free. Stage-III organisations, as we have noted, engage people's souls. That's powerful! Because they feel such a deep level of involvement in the business and little unmanageable fear, people have little difficulty "doing whatever needs to be done".[30]

Perhaps the greatest change in the behavioural communication patterns would be seen in the area of feedback: *appreciate* behaviour and very specific asks. People sincerely motivated to improve the quality of any relationship must be continuously aware of their own behaviour and consequences. Until an organisation is at Stage III, where members see themselves as being in partnership, the person in the high-power position must take the lead in periodically *asking*, "How is my behaviour affecting the quality of our relationship from your point of view?" "What am I doing, intentionally or not, that could lead you to conclude that I do not care for you?"

It will take time to overcome the anxiety and fear associated with an authority asking this question *and* a patient (in the broadest sense of the word), answering it with assertive authority.

Physicians will maintain their expert power over matters of technical quality. Patients have expertise over a different domain. Lacking medical competence, patients "must rely on the affective dimension [TLC] of the doctor-patient relationship in evaluating the physician's role performances".[31] But over time, it is this feedback process that is the lifeblood of change and growth in any relationship. Without feedback there is no growing up, no increasing teamwork.

The more the ambiguity, the greater the fear and anxiety we feel. The bridge we must have, especially during transitions, is the helping hand of staying in touch, feeling the pulse. The greater the ambiguity, the closer must be the contact, just as ships in a fog must sound their horns more frequently.

When the sailing got rough at the Nalle Clinic, trusted physician colleagues jumped ship. An observer commented, "All they're thinking

---

[29] See p. 69.
[30] See p. 29 for further discussion of attaining organisational excellence.
[31] Press, p. 67.

about is what's going to be important to them, no matter who they step on or let down".[32]

TLC without all the available technology will only prolong patient suffering. On the other hand, technology without the power of TLC carries little hope for the healing profession to be able to first heal itself.[33]

Our only hope may lie in the hands and hearts of men and women like Dr. Ray Fernandez who have the courage to struggle to guide their institutions through the turbulent passages of growing up.

> So the stage is set for the most familiar confrontation of modern life—between people who demand change and institutions who resist it. The institutions alter, but never fast enough, and those who seek change are bitterly disappointed.
>
> In the resulting conflict we find our institutions in a savage crossfire between uncritical lovers and unloving critics. On the one side those who love their institutions tend to smother them in an embrace of death. On the other side there has arisen a breed of critics without love, skilled in demolition and untutored in the arts by which human institutions are nurtured and strengthened and made to flourish. Where human institutions are concerned, love without criticism brings stagnation and criticism without love brings destruction. The swifter the pace of change, the more lovingly men must care for and criticise their institutions to keep them intact through the turbulent passages.[34]

---

[32] See p. 112 for full quotation.
[33] For a discussion of technology and TLC, high tech/high touch, see John Naisbitt, *Megatrends: Ten New Directions Transforming Our Lives*, (New York: Warner Books, 1982).
[34] John Gardner, *Recovery of Confidence*, (New York: W.W. Norton Co., Inc., 1970), pp. 29–30.

Part Four

Closure and prognosis

Chart entry

Endings and beginnings

Irwin Rubin, PhD

A TRANSFORMATION THAT began years ago—that had allowed Dr. Fernandez to accept an entire organisation of providers as his primary-care patients—was entering its next stage. His struggle to accept the painful realisation that he was about to become the first former physician-CEO of the Nalle Clinic reflects the human experience of death and dying at two levels: the first, the loss of title or position, seemed minor next to the second. The really painful deaths are those associated with losing the respect and friendship of longstanding colleagues. Following one's heart and doing what you deeply believe is best for the welfare of the whole will not always result in remaining popular. To better understand this aspect of leadership, we will need to draw lessons from the agony of defeat as well as from the thrill of victory. To broaden our conscious awareness and insight, we must venture into what Jung calls the shadow side of our own personalities.

I made a special effort to stay in touch with Dr. Fernandez during this period of turmoil and upheaval, a period he anticipated, although he did not anticipate its emotional intensity. He describes it in the closing paragraph of his personal chart entry of 5 December 1988:

> The highs are higher and the lows lower in my current position than in medical practice. As patients literally put their lives in their physician's hands, so the life of the organisation is in mine. The challenge of controlling a complex organisation's culture, financial performance, quality control, and morale is exciting. As the organisation progresses through change and growth, I take a parent's pride in its successes. Still, the fear and frustration of dealing with the unknown is something physician-managers have to live with every day. Like Columbus, we have to realise that most people actually hope we'll fall off the end of the world so that they can remain secure in their

belief that the world is flat, and that physicians do not make good administrators.

In addition to wanting to support an old friend and colleague, I knew from my experience and training that some of the hostility towards him reflected normal transference dynamics of the leadership process. When your patient is a gangling adolescent, you expect and recognise the need for an intense period of counter-dependence. He'll sass you and think you're from the Stone Age, but you realise that it's all part of his process of accepting responsibilities and becoming an interdependent adult. As John Gardner recently put it in an interview, "For any leader, there is an absolutely unresolvable tension between the responsibilities to those he or she leads, and the responsibilities to the greater good". As a consequence, Gardner concludes, one of the unrecognised qualities leaders must develop is the capacity to absorb hostility, "to learn not to take it personally, to realise the criticism is aimed at the office, not at them".[35]

However, while the rational mind knows that the child must struggle to make its own way, the heart still experiences the pain of the separation. In a 24 January 1990, letter, Dr. Fernandez expressed his feelings: "Tough time to go through right now—feelings of loneliness, lack of appreciation, confusion, and failure. Must be like living through a divorce!" The emotional closeness, the bonding which takes place between physician and patient, was beginning to shift. In addition, colleagues who disagreed with his leadership were jumping ship, taking valued affiliations, business and personal, with them. The image of divorce aptly captures this process. Long after the formal decrees are signed, it's painful when divorced partners bump into one another.

In January 1990 the discontent at the Nalle Clinic received a public airing. Dr. Fernandez wrote, "Have included a few clippings FYI [for your information]. [Quotes from *Business Journal* and *Observer* appear in commentary in Part Three.] Media isn't *helping* me to keep morale and trust up! Got to admit that this is the low point of an otherwise fine career in management. Interesting to observe how some 'old friends' ignore the painful situation, others simply acknowledge it, and others express concern and support".

To come to terms with the feeling that he was losing his patient and valued colleagues—the pain of impending divorce, to which he previously referred—I suggested to Dr. Fernandez that he talk about these feelings with his wife and that he tape-record these conversations. The chart entries I have selected for this fourth part of our clinical analysis

---

[35] Joe Flower, "The Role of the Leader", *Healthcare Forum Journal*, May/June 1990, p. 33.

will be brief excerpts from private encounters between Dr. and Mrs. Fernandez. As readers, we are privileged to glimpse these conversations, for they can help us see aspects of the leadership process that we might overlook.

I must approach my interpretive commentary, which I will interweave with the chart entries rather than following our previous format, even more cautiously than in Part Two. As you have become aware, my psychological bias is Jungian. In this context, for any healing to be complete, masculine and feminine perceptions must be in harmony. In the Jungian sense, these terms reflect archetypal qualities in every person—not gender-specific qualities. That means, each of us is a composite of intellect and feeling, intuition and rational thought, toughness and softness, masculine and feminine. Conscious awareness of new beginnings and endings often resonate as the stirring of feelings arising from the feminine. We are fortunate to be able to include in our final chart entries the perspectives from Mrs. Gail Fernandez. She's a catalyst, a behind-the-scenes confidante, and a supporter of his transformation from physician to physician-manager to physician-CEO.

Early in the first of these conversations, Mrs. Fernandez is recounting a phone conversation she had with the wife of a physician who had just announced his resignation from the Clinic. While having "no hard feelings against" the husband's needing to "go his own way", Mrs. Fernandez also "felt a real sense of lack of loyalty". In spite of the thought that "I'm sure they're the same people", she reported that the quality of their relationship "seems to have changed. As a result, I had a strained feeling". Mrs. Fernandez, too, has lost an old friendship.

The masculine part of ourselves that allows us to feel married to a career might find it difficult to maintain psychic boundaries between achievement and affiliation, between business and friendship. (In our society, this part is usually stronger in men.) The feminine side (which is usually stronger in women), typically puts relationships before personal achievement. Mrs. Fernandez reports that "these problems have not been as difficult for me [as they were for Dr. Fernandez]. I've been able, for the most part, to separate clinic from personal. Most of my friends have been able to see me apart from the Clinic problems of their spouses. Two or three friendships have, unfortunately, been totally ended—on their part, not mine".

When we betray the precarious psychic balance between our short-term self-interest and our joint commitment to a long-term relationship, our feminine side screams out. If we violate our own values on the path to success, our success feels meaningless. We sit at the top, empty. The process of leadership carries both the joys of life and the pains of death.

In exploring more deeply her own unease regarding physicians who deserted during the time of stress, Mrs. Fernandez comments to her husband,

> I just feel like they were looking out for their own benefit, which I guess I can't fault them with. But they jumped ship, not thinking about how the rest of us felt that were still a part of the Nalle Clinic, but just concerned to look out for themselves. And to me, in a nutshell, that's what's happening: these guys aren't looking at a group practice, or a clinic that they need to be loyal to as players of a team. All they're thinking about is what's going to be important to them— no matter who they step on or let down.

> Well, I'm sure they blame you. I'm sure they've said many harsh words about you in their homes or with whoever they can talk to about the Clinic. That's hard for me to understand, because you're a tool of the Clinic. You're only an agent of the Clinic who's supposed to carry out its mission. So I can't understand why it's your fault.

In labelling the fears lurking in the shadow of her husband's psyche— the possibility, horrifying to any physician, that he might have been guilty of malpractice in the care of his patient—and in bringing out into the open words others spoke in the shadows behind his back, Mrs. Fernandez enables Dr. Fernandez to begin the painful acceptance of his new role, with its diminished responsibilities and authority. Just as his colleagues felt he had betrayed them when he moved from physician to physician-manager to physician-CEO, he now feels his patient is betraying *him* as it moves away from him.

The first stages in dealing with death and dying—denial and anger— become immediately accessible to the psyche when the feminine can speak so the masculine can hear. Dr. Fernandez writes,

> They pushed me.... They gave me the helm of this ship, albeit not a very seaworthy craft. They forget the fact that what they're asking for is unreasonable, or perhaps even impossible to accomplish [*just as, in the heat of the moment, Dr. Fernandez forgets the fact that he took the helm without a clear job description or a set of performance indicators*]. They don't realise that the captain needs money, staff, and the support of a crew to sail.

Notwithstanding that the criticism is not personal but a part of the turf (leaving aside the question of whether it is justifiable), it hurts. Denial and anger are natural human responses. Learning to deal with hostility does not mean becoming impervious to the pain, for then leaders risk losing the acute sensitivity necessary to feel the pulse of their constituency. The leader must manage the pain and find safe outlets for discharging it.

Sensitive to Dr. Fernandez's anger and hurt, and with the feminine's sense of our inherent interdependence, Mrs. Fernandez reminds him of the impossibility of sailing a ship when "everybody's jumping overboard". "It can't be done overnight," she adds, especially "when they don't give you all the essential tools." The feminine knows well that children grow up only in their own time, requiring constant attention, feeding, and nurturing.

Feeling "like a failure, like I'm not doing a good job" begins to come into balance with Dr. Fernandez's ability to see and accept what he is experiencing. He gets conscious and unconscious contradictory messages: on the one hand, that he "is important, that the organisation recognises and knows it needs its leader"; on the other hand, this same organisation says, "We don't want you; it's time for a new administration."

As Dr. Fernandez becomes painfully aware, leadership during periods of cultural transition is full of mixed signals saying, "You're damned if you do and damned if you don't." Realising that it's not personal enables him to resist the temptation to "bail out ... go on and do something else that might feel personally better". Instead, he realises that quality patient care means eliminating himself as physician-CEO. In other words, he refers his patient, the Nalle Clinic, to another specialist.

This phase of leadership in organisational cultural change is physically and emotionally demanding. There are tough settlements to make. The impending joint venture with PhyCor—the transition to a Stage-II business organisation—requires Dr. Fernandez to negotiate termination agreements with valued colleagues and old friends who did not choose to stay with PhyCor. We can understand that physicians are reluctant to perform complicated surgery on family and close friends. Similarly, when your patient is an entire organisation in the midst of cultural change, in the "turning over of the reins of management and decision-making to new people", you will inevitably and reluctantly have to tell some dear, old friends that their membership is terminal. Whispered rumours, totally unfounded, that those in leadership positions are accepting under-the-table sweeteners do not make the dirty work of leadership any easier. The feminine jumps to the fore at this point, and Mrs. Fernandez labels that dynamic for what it is, a natural projection from shadows of anxious psyches: "That's their motivation, but that is not your motivation." Thus, although he finds this pettiness frustrating, Dr. Fernandez is able to acknowledge, "I guess there's no surprise."

As we bring this clinical case to a close, I must reemphasise a point I made in the commentary to Part Two: "[I]t is individuals who act as leaders. Whether or not these initiatives are mutually beneficial, and at what costs to whom, depend on the quality of the exchange. The quality of the partnership, the relationship between a patient and a provider, determines the outcome of healing."

Just as pieces of Dr. Fernandez's self-image had to change in order for him to transform his commitment to patient care to an entire organisation, so, too, the organisation—his patient—had to experience the loss of an old identity to take on a new one. Both parties to the leadership relationship have to experience their versions of the natural cycles of beginnings and endings. Although we read Dr. Benedum's view in the commentaries in Part Three, we do not know how the entire patient-organisation would describe its experiences of leadership and organisational cultural change as it struggled to grow up.

We do know that 48 hours after the PhyCor negotiations closed, a previously scheduled Nalle Clinic annual party took place. The timing of this symbolic act of breaking bread, which Dr. Fernandez attributes to "just an absolute stroke of providence", Jung would have seen as pure synchronicity.

Instead of the depression of the past few months, Dr. Fernandez reports an "amazing turn when people knew where we were going.... There was no longer any question about who was in and who was out". A renewed sense of pride seemed to surge through the patient, a feeling as if "we had really succeeded almost beyond our wildest dreams". Handshaking and back patting replaced finger pointing and back stabbing. People were "starting to smile again". Even the press acknowledged the positive momentum that had begun. Within two months, a prestigious family-practice group of eleven physicians in four satellites joined the Clinic.

Even the solitary individual who, in the face of growing dissension and desertion, had led the patient where the patient wanted to go[36] reported "actually getting ... some congratulations". One of his colleagues captured the essence of leadership (the dirty work) in organisational cultural change, when he congratulated Dr. Fernandez on being able "to turn chicken shit into chicken salad".

---

[36] 99.5% of the Clinic's physicians voted to sell their shares to PhyCor.

Epilogue

Writing on the perils of detachment in the health-care industry, Emily Friedman describes the "basic conflict of the care giver: 'How can I be compassionate without becoming so involved that I cannot bear the suffering?'" She warns us, "When patients cease to be people, everything is lost".[37] Living on the horns of this dilemma—when your patient is an entire organisation—is one of the leadership challenges. In this unedited last paragraph of the tape dictated several days after the annual party, Dr. Fernandez reminds us all of the essential lesson of humility at the core of leadership and organisational cultural change.

> I guess it must be like the general in times of war having to order some of his troops to storm the hill, absolutely knowing full well in advance that a lot of them are going to get shot and killed. When knowing that that's what's necessary to win the war: you've got to lose some of your people in battle. I guess still the general doesn't sleep very well at night, knowing that his command is what causes a lot of very, very personal suffering. Even though maybe it's his army that ultimately prevails and wins the war.

---

[37] "The Perils of Detachment", *Healthcare Forum Journal*, March/April 1990, p. 10.

Commentary

"What's it all about, Alfie?"

Dr. Raymond Fernandez
August 1990

WHAT DOES ALL this change and the effect that it had on me and the organisation really mean? What are the lessons here? Those close to me are asking how things are going now, six months into a very new structure at the Clinic. To a casual observer, my role has changed significantly. But candidly, in a crucial way it hasn't changed at all. I have always been asked to be an interpreter and a commentator. A crucial duty I have performed all along is to help those around me who were actually performing the work of the organisation to understand what the organisation is doing and how their role is meaningful. Right now that interpreter's function is more crucial than ever.

Not only my role, but everyone's role in the organisation has changed. I'm but an indicator of how things are. It's a truism that during times of transition and evolution, those in the middle of change may have a hard time seeing that things are changing around them. The many false starts and brief stops of our organisation, when viewed over a continuum of time, have been very hard emotionally on the individuals primarily involved in those changes. But physicians always see their patients episodically. A patient's only doctor visit for a while might be for an annual physical examination. If so, the physician can easily lose sight that the patient has a life between doctor visits and, indeed, that that individual's life is outside of the doctor's office. The sick patient who is hospitalised again is visited only briefly and episodically by the physician. It is only over the continuum of years that the patient's true health status can be assessed. The physician easily gets emotionally involved and empathic with the patient during times of diagnosed crises. But the best role for the physician and patient can only be worked out when the physician sees the patient's life moving forward—occasionally with assistance from the physician, sometimes in spite of the physician, but most importantly, progressing best when the patient takes on responsibility for his or her own health. Both doctor and patient must resist the temptation that the patient become dependent on the physician.

It was in September of 1989 that maximum stresses were occurring within the organisation. I can't help but recall the ironic analogy that struck Charlotte, North Carolina at that same time in the form of Hurricane Hugo. This was one of the most devastating storms to hit the United States in history. Who could have expected so much destruction, especially 200 miles inland? The city of Charlotte was left without electricity for weeks, with a snarled transportation system, inability of businesses to open their doors, and untold property damage. One of Charlotte's proudest assets is its stately trees, and fully 25% of them were lost. The unexpected tempest resulted in loss of all the weaker trees. Those with a deep, strong root system endured and now prosper. But the temporary change in the topography was soon cleared and the scars left on a lovely city were removed by the proud citizens who remained and rolled up their sleeves.

The Clinic used its internal tempest as a time to restructure, reassess, and refocus. An outside agency (PhyCor) served as the necessary emergency vehicle that came to the assistance of a neighbour. PhyCor represented an outside resource that could be called upon to help make certain needed changes and to shore up certain bent, but not broken, trees. The Clinic had previously been thinking of a new structure to improve decision making and to promote leadership. It had brought non-physicians onto its Board of Directors. It was considering giving ownership over to a tax-free foundation. It had recognised its adolescent growing pains. It only required—and, indeed, provided itself—an emergency to force actions that might otherwise have been postponed.

Now six months into a new structure, it is obvious that certain goals that eluded us in the past could now be accomplished almost with ease. We have changed our compensation formula. We have altered pension benefits to be more realistic. A reserve fund is established, and a profit margin is being obtained. Marketing is being planned in earnest.

Physicians now feel a much greater sense of security than they have had in a good while. They are able to get back to the basics. Their concentration is now on practising medicine, and they have more confidence that the administrative aspects and the control of overhead will be taken care of. They don't find it necessary to have the direct personal involvement in this, as they did before. Thus, the physicians have given up some of their control. But the trade-off has more than made up for any loss. Physicians now feel comfortable going about their primary task of providing medical services to patients.

My personal sense through this is that I, too, have given up a large element of control of the Clinic. It is a pleasure watching us being more successful than ever before. It's as though now I'm watching someone else being successful at something I started. The patient that was last seen in intensive care and had to be referred out to a specialist is now back in full health. There is a sense of pride that now we are meeting certain goals that had to be met. That accomplishment is much more important than bickering about which administration is accomplishing it.

Editor's note: In a tape he dictated just prior to the manuscript's going to press, Dr. Fernandez provided an additional and critical insight as to an important and normal aspect of what this process of organisational growing up is all about. For six weeks he had pushed for an annual performance evaluation (critical, as we noted earlier, to the growing-up process), in his continuing role as full-time Medical Director.

"The two officers [of the Board] assigned the task of doing this job", he reports, "gave me an excellent evaluation". In their proposal to the Board, however, they were going to recommend "that the amount of time devoted by the Medical Director to administrative duties should decrease from 'a full-time job' to 65 percent". In addition to finding that personally unacceptable, Dr. Fernandez knew that such regression, while not unusual, was potentially dangerous: "It seemed to me like a patient who was over an acute illness and no longer in pain, jumping to the conclusion that they didn't need as much medical care."

In no uncertain terms, Dr. Fernandez informed his patient of the risks involved. "I pointed out that it is premature to declare victory", that in spite of the essential support that PhyCor offered, "it would be a step backward to diminish the time, knowledge, energy, and commitment of the Clinic to promoting its own internal systems [to growing up]". The Medical Director, Dr. Fernandez stressed, "functions as a personification of the Board of Directors itself and represents the spirit of the leadership team". To diminish the role—as a principle, independent of personalities—he warns the patient, "would be to diminish the role of the Board of Directors and the entire leadership of the Clinic". Such loving toughness, though difficult to manifest, is absolutely essential. Fortunately, it "got their attention", for after a "vigorous discussion, the Board unanimously reaffirmed that they still want a full-time Medical Director with appropriate compensation".

This little vignette confirms what we knew all along about the process of growing up. Perfection (perfect health) is an abstraction that lives only in mythology. Physical, emotional, intellectual, and spiritual progress is all we humans can claim. As Dr. Fernandez concluded, "The battle is never really over."

Commentary

Human parallels to organisational development

Irwin Rubin, PhD

IN THE Nalle Clinic we can find many human parallels to normal organisational development as I have described it in the commentary "Organisations Have to Grow Up". I don't know of any widely accepted, empirically verified model of the growth stages that people in organisations go through. The mission of the health-care industry depends on a human process. Skilled professionals use all human and technological means available to heal patients. Humanisation of this industry is not (as might be true in the automobile industry, for example), simply a matter of altruism ("It's good to be good to people"), or business profitability. When the bottom line is healing, treating people with TLC (tender love and care), is essential. Humanness in health care is the heart and soul of the business. Humanness is the values and behaviours that inspire commitment to quality care, to healing. A humanistic model of organisational development in health care could contribute to the development of a more humanistic industry and higher-quality patient care.

There is an intimate relationship between the organisations that comprise an industry and the industry as a whole. By examining the development of the Nalle Clinic, we can see what is going on in other organisations and in the health-care industry. (Similarly, by looking at these, we can learn about other industries.) Both the Clinic and the health-care industry mature through a series of stages. Both have a mission or direction. Both must re-examine their fundamental purpose. Until this mission work is completed, neither will be able to develop new solutions to problems of structure and procedure.

In labelling a Stage-I health-care organisation as having a "childlike orientation", I did not mean to suggest that individual members are themselves childlike. They are seriously dedicated to the care of patients. The term describes the quality of the relationships, particularly among the physicians and between them and their parent organisation. I do not use it judgementally; I use it to describe a normal developmental process. Learning to walk is a prerequisite to gaining the strength, balance, and sense of purpose, to run.

Within Maslow's developmental hierarchy of human motivation, the parent organisation provides the fraternity membership a roof overhead, food on the table, and protection against external threat, particularly these days from the legal fraternity. Consistent with the spirit of a childlike orientation, the members of the fraternity expect to receive these benefits at the lowest possible cost. They resist spending for the long-term improvement of the frat house because to do so would mean fewer dollars to gratify their personal needs now.

Once there was a physician who fancied himself as a medical George Patton, complete with "a pearl-handled stethoscope". He imagined he could lead his fraternal colleagues onto innovative beachheads in medicine. Any readers with teenagers will recognise their own family dynamic in his description of the difference between reality and fantasy:

> He said the difference between the Patton image and the reality of his medical leadership could be exemplified by a typical meeting in which (1) three of the people critical to the meeting and whom he counted on to provide support would arrive late; (2) two other key physicians would argue vigorously against the concept that he was proposing; (3) several other physicians indicated that they would not be at all interested in participating in the programme; and (4) one physician would indicate that unless he was authorised to expend more money on specialised equipment for traditional programmes, he would not participate in any new efforts by the organisation (but would be willing to head a committee to organise the purchase of the equipment).[38]

We never resolve our developmental issues once and for all. They keep coming back. Discussing the psychosocial hurdles we must clear during our lives, Erikson carefully points out that new experiences will unsettle once-satisfactory levels of developmental achievement.[39] For example, while learning a new skill, adults naturally feel like babes in

---

[38] André L. Delbecq and Sandra L. Gill, "Justice as a Prelude to Teamwork in Medical Centers", *HCM Review*, Winter, 1985, p. 46.
[39] Erik Erikson, *Childhood and Society*, Second Edition, (New York: W.W. Norton & Company, Inc., 1964).

the woods. In Erikson's terms, we will re-experience the autonomy challenge, which we first confronted in our childhood. Similarly, seriously
ill patients will feel the fear and dependency that go along with the basic
trust hurdle we all faced in infancy.

This notion of natural regression helps us understand the developmental challenges that health-care faces as an industry. In Erikson's
framework, organised medicine is in its infancy or early childhood.
Whereas individual professionals have passed at least once through
many of Erikson's stages, the industry as a whole has not yet done so.

George Bernard Shaw noted, "The tragedy of illness at present is that
it delivers you helplessly into the hands of a profession which you
deeply mistrust". This comment speaks directly to Erikson's first developmental challenge of infancy, the trust issue. The idea that the "air of
the operating room, where once the doctor was sovereign, is now so
dense with the second guesses of insurers, regulators, lawyers, consultants, and risk managers that the physician has little room to breathe,
much less heal", speaks directly to Erikson's second developmental
challenge of autonomy. The *Time* magazine article that reported these
comments was quick to point out that "the soreness may also reflect the
stresses and strains of a profession in transition".[40]

Individuals cannot detour around developmental hurdles. If we try to
stay put, we risk stagnating. The same is true for health-care organisations and the industry they are a part of. Group-practice organisations,
in particular, will have to work through some aspects of the fraternity
model. This training will develop the strength and perspective necessary
to become a Stage-II business organisation.

While each organisation must chart its own course through Stage II,
the waters have been navigated before. And many have lived to tell and
write the tale. The basic business organisation is a highly researched,
well-documented organism. Scientists have done much ground-breaking
research on adult roles, needs, and performance. Seasoned travellers
offer regular training through health-care associations.

I don't doubt that the health-care industry will rise to the challenges
of adolescence and young adulthood and get down to business. But the
real challenge is yet to come. An industry whose fundamental mission
requires individual members to "give up a piece of their *souls*—to invest
their *selves* in the business"—has no choice but to become replete with
Stage-III organisations. It's not enough for the health-care industry to

---

[40] Nancy Gibbs, "Sick and Tired", *Time*, 31 July 1989, pp. 48–9.

have well-run businesses. No, not in a healing profession. As I said earlier, the search for excellence is the foundation of the entire profession of medicine. Physicians are always working to improve patient care with a more effective laser, antibiotic, or diet. Continuous improvement is equally critical when the patient is an entire organisation of providers.

Because the industry is young, few Stage-III organisations are available for study, although many organisations are preparing themselves for the push to the next plateau. Deming-and-Juran-type projects, which focus on technical quality assurance and cost savings, can contribute to creating strong Stage-II health-care organisations. In my experience, their left-brain focus does not speak to the non-linear, quantum leap in consciousness necessary to propel us into the search for excellence. Both the quality and the discussion of the information that individuals contribute in their quality circles rest upon the highest levels of trust. While Deming's steps refer to the need to reduce fear, in my own experience, few organisations treat this issue with the attention it deserves.

Health-care institutions exist to fulfil two functions: curative and healing. Curing requires technical effectiveness (trained providers performing skilfully) and managerial efficiency (the organisation must survive financially to fulfil any function). Healing, by contrast, requires love and nurturance, heart and soul (versus mind and matter). Total quality care is a function of three factors: effectiveness, efficiency, and TLC.

Continuous improvement through experiential learning requires overcoming the debilitating effects of fear and anxiety. Just as the fear of dying can sap a patient's strength and will to live, the fear of negative treatment from within the organisation can sap a provider's strength and capacity to care. For example, a board of trustees that removes a CEO in an inhumane manner, and thus traumatises the provider organisation, can infect the healing culture of its organisation. And angry physicians who verbally abuse nursing staff (or medical students, as recent research[41] has suggested), may be guilty of behavioural malpractice as poisonous, and as avoidable, as staph infections in the operating room.

Love and nurturance, the seeds from which healing experiences grow, are human commodities that health-care institutions must produce before they can share. Like other treasured natural resources, TLC is not a commodity that we can abuse without replenishing. We can't buy

---

[41] Silver and Glicken, pp. 527–537.

it and stock it on the shelf. It must be given freely and, like a child's spontaneity, it will only be sustained by an environment free of unwarranted fear and anxiety, by a healing culture.[42] As St. Marguerite Hospital in Japan has learned, treating patients, be they individuals or organisations, with TLC is the way to reduce fear.

The search for excellence requires continuous learning from experience. Still, each succeeding cycle will confront new and unfamiliar territory. Unless we regularly experience feeling like "babes in the woods", we cannot be certain we are sailing, as Columbus did, on heretofore uncharted waters. If we are, we need new skills. Our lunar astronauts faced this Columbus-like challenge. No human experience existed that would help them prepare for a forced landing on the dark side of the moon, cut off from earth communication. Training for that possibility involved learning how to use consensual decision-making (as opposed to traditionally relying on their commander) to become map makers. Map reading skills would have been useless in an emergency.

This line of thinking aligns the challenges of human development and organisational development. First, the very fear and anxiety that patients experience when they are seriously ill is no different from the fear and anxiety that health-care organisations experience as they set sail in search of excellence. Second, just as self-actualisation is an ideal in human development, excellence is an ideal in organisational development.

In an article about the respected medical futurist Leland Kaiser, Wesley Curry writes,

> A paradox for the next century will be that, as we move to high technology, we will also move to high touch.... One of the important distinctions to make in the years ahead in terms of medical care is the difference between curing and healing.... Curing is a problem for medical science. Healing is a problem of human love and nurturance....

> Dr. Kaiser expects healing to play a greater role in the system in the future. "I think the hospital of the future will say that it heals everyone who comes through its doors. Those it can cure, it cures." Dr. Kaiser calls this new hospital an "experiential organisation". He says that it provides a "transforming experience" for the patient.[43]

---

[42] Excerpted from an unpublished article by Irwin Rubin, "Managing Fear and Its Effects on the Quality of Care", copyright 1990 by Temenos®, Inc., USA.
[43] Wesley Curry, "Looking Ahead", *Physician Executive*, 16, no. 1, (January–February 1990), p. 4.

According to our fundamental premise, the health-care organisation of the future will provide a "transforming experience" for patients only to the extent that it provides a transforming experience for its own members. To enhance the quality of the healing experience the industry offers patients, it will first have to heal itself. I don't mean to imply a current state of illness; rather, I am speaking of yet another attempt to grow up.

Malpractice mania is rampant. As a result, many practising physicians feel despair, wishing they had never gone into medicine in the first place. With college students choosing other professions, medical-school enrolments have dropped. While these industry trends are painful, they can signal a basic, and ultimately strengthening, developmental transition.

What will it take to grow up? First, Erikson's challenge to the medical industry involves a willingness to reach out and seek enrichment from its patients. He says that humans are a teaching and a learning animal.[44] Part of the problem of mistrust between physicians and patients is that there hasn't been enough give and take. So far, it's been mostly give from the physicians and mostly take from the patients. Just as parents learn from and teach their children, providers and patients are interdependent, too. While we cannot, and should not, expect lay patients to be able to judge the quality of the technical care they receive, the patients should be the final authority on the quality of the human care they receive.

Second, there must be a healing attitude—by this I mean human love and nurturance—in the whole organisation: among administrators, physicians, and staff. (In the past, the healing attitude has usually been from physicians towards their patients.) The adversarial attitude between administrators has made it difficult for physicians to treat their patients with love and nurturance. A squabble in the meeting room does not make for kindness in the treatment room. Providers who, in the short run, manage to put squabbles out of their minds and to be the ideal healers to their patients, face early burnout. TLC is a human commodity that a health-care organisation must generate before it can export it to patients. As Emily Friedman warned, "When patients cease to be people, everything is lost."[45] We must remember the plaque outside St. Marguerite Hospital that promises:

---

[44] Erikson, p. 216.
[45] Friedman, p. 10.

To heal sometimes
To support often
To comfort always

George Bernard Shaw's comment, referred to earlier, that "The tragedy of illness at present is that it delivers you helplessly into the hands of professionals you deeply mistrust" challenges the health-care industry to regain a rapidly eroding sense of integrity. Integrity means keeping its mission in mind—that is, being primarily concerned with the patient's well being. I remember our family doctor, who brought me into the world and all my sisters, too. He was *our* doctor. My parents wouldn't have dreamed of suing him, because they knew how much he cared for us. Nowadays, some patients think their doctors care more for money. Patients wonder why they're being sent for another test. Perhaps his colleagues need the business? Perhaps the doctor is practising defensive medicine, fearing a lawsuit? In either case, the motive for the test is not believed to be love for the patient. To rise to a Stage-III organisation, to self-actualise, means, in Erikson's terms, to win another round in the constant human battle of despair vs. ego integrity. An industry that possesses integrity "is ready to defend the dignity of its own mission against all physical and economic threats".[46]

What will happen to organisations that do not choose to change? Staying in Stage I means remaining a fraternity, at least for a while. Obsolescence is the most likely long-term consequence. Stagnation in Stage II is not likely to be fatal to the organisation. Neither will it result in the fullest healing of its patients.

By developing a humanistic organisational paradigm that acknowledges the essential oneness of human development with organisational development, the health-care industry has the opportunity to contribute to the health of the nation.

---

[46] Erikson, p. 268.

Part Five

Autopsy

Post-mortem postscript

The demise of the Nalle Clinic[1]

Jeremiah H. Holleman, MD

Patient: The Nalle Clinic
Subject: An autopsy report

Editor's note: A health care organisation exists to provide the highest quality of patient care humanly possible. In an effort to help health care organisations meet this challenge, the preceding chapters of *My Pulse*—using the Nalle Clinic as clinical case example—have stressed two fundamental points:

1. A health care organisation is a living, breathing human organism. It is born, experiences patterns of normal growing pains, and copes with times of joy, fear, sadness, and threat. As such, a health care organisation can (and, indeed, must) be viewed as analogous to a Patient.
2. The quality of care a patient can hope to experience in the organisation's treatment rooms is directly related to the quality of care the Patient organisation receives from those upon whose shoulders falls the responsibility to care for the human organism that itself cares for patients. Raising awareness of the Patient's need for TLC is the **leadership challenge** involved in keeping a health care organisation's pulse strongly beating.

However, as the recent events have sadly proven, a human organism, a Patient organisation that "seemed to be the embodiment of success...highly regarded by

---

[1] Dr. Jeremiah Holleman, Jr., M.D., "The Demise of the Nalle Clinic" *The Physician Executive,* January– February 2001, pages 26–31 (Used with permission from the ACPE and Dr. Jeremiah Holleman, Jr.)

[both] the medical community and by patients" is no more immortal than its individual human elements. On 30 April 2000, after 79 years of operation, the Nalle Clinic closed its doors. The Patient died and hundreds of thousands of patients lost their provider of care.

Two physician CEOs were the Nalle Clinic's "Attendings" during its last dozen or so years of life. Dr. Ray Fernandez, as you've read, held that position from the late 1980s until 1995 when Dr. Jeremiah Holleman. Jr.—in conjunction with the contractual business management arrangement signed into effect with PhyCor—assumed that responsibility until the Patient's pulse stopped beating. Dr. Holleman courageously published his own autopsy assessment. In addition to Dr. Fernandez's retrospective autopsy reflections, Dr. Holleman's thoughts follow in their entirety.

My goal in the following commentaries is to support Drs. Fernandez and Holleman. As physicians, they are doing what they were trained to do. For this same kind of post-mortem assessment is one of the health care profession's most sacred tenets: when a patient dies unexpectedly, learning why is vital to protect others from the same fate.

Having said that, we are immediately confronted with a paradox. For if an organisation is a living breathing human organism, a Patient's death—however painful and sad—may be a natural and inevitable outcome of living. "Old age" or "natural causes" are seldom seen as the noted cause of death on a patient's death certificate. Rather, we feel impelled to provide a label which carries the subtle implication that if we had been able to cure the patient's "pneumonia", for example, that they might have lived on. Forever.

Whether or not the Nalle Clinic should have or could have continued to live on, there is still much to be learned from stepping back and exploring the kinds of questions Drs. Holleman and Fernandez so poignantly raise.

THREE ASSOCIATES joined Brodie Nalle, MD, in 1921 to form the Nalle Clinic, which prospered and slowly grew. By 1961, there were 14 physicians occupying a new building. In 1975, the first primary care satellite was established. The clinic functioned largely as a condominium model and was recognised as a strong organisation with an emphasis on speciality medicine and surgical care. By the early 80s, with many other medical and surgical specialists entering the market, Nalle developed a primary care network and opened new satellites.

The governance through the mid-80s was a true democracy, with a large board deferring important decisions to the staff. Monthly staff meetings were usually acrimonious and lasted late into the night. It became clear that we were not able to make decisions quickly enough to respond to the changing environment. In the late 80s, under the leadership of medical director Ray Fernandez, MD, Nalle moved to a smaller, stronger board, which was empowered to make most management decisions.

By 1989 we were making better, faster decisions—but we continued to struggle with the environment, collections, business functions, and profitability. In 1990, we signed a contract with a new, little known practice management company named PhyCor, headquartered in Nashville, Tennessee. Both PhyCor and Nalle had the naïve intention that the physicians would practice medicine, PhyCor would run the business, and the Joint Policy Board, with members of both organisations, would deal with mutual issues, such as strategy, fees, and satellite locations.

Little did we realise that there were almost no issues that were either purely practice or business. Rather, every medical decision impacted the business, and every business decision affected the practice of medicine. Our agreement called for PhyCor to manage accounts receivable, human resources, and other general business functions, as well as provide access to capital. In exchange for these services, PhyCor received a percentage of the profits. In the early 90s, the arrangement seemed to be mutually beneficial. Physician compensation was up, collections increased, relations with our hospital partner improved, we grew rapidly to 140 physicians, and, in 1995, moved into a beautiful, new building.

How could this happen?

By 1998 the skies had darkened, and those of us on the inside knew trouble lay ahead. On 30 April 2000, after 79 years of operation, the Nalle Clinic closed its doors. The 140-physician multi speciality clinic had seemed to be the embodiment of success and was one of the major players in the Charlotte, North Carolina health care arena.

The initial reaction was a combination of surprise, sadness, and anger. And then, Why? How could this happen? What happened? What went wrong? Could other health care organisations suffer the same fate? As President of Nalle for the past six years, I was in the midst of what was successful, as well as unsuccessful. On the other hand, it is difficult to be totally objective in describing circumstances in which one is a part. This article, therefore, has the strengths and weaknesses of an insider's view of the trials and tribulations of the clinic's last days.

Across the US, health care organisations are struggling in this turbulent environment characterised by increased expenses, decreased reimbursement, and more regulatory pressures. Decreasing reimbursement for services by health plans and Medicare is familiar to all of us. One of our physicians recently showed me copies of his 1988 and 2000 Medicare fee schedules—for many surgical codes, fees were half of what they had been in 1988.

Health plans, pressure from employers, Medicare, and the effects of the BBA'97 are putting downward pressure on reimbursement. The vigorous national economy, growing communities, and low unemployment are putting upward pressure on personnel and real estate expenses. The increasing complexity and diversity of health plans requires more sophisticated billing and computer systems for all health care providers.

But there were characteristics specific to Nalle that made it particularly difficult for us to manage in this environment. With decreased reimbursement and increased cost, our fate was somewhat predictable—we experienced a steady decline in profitability in recent years, resulting in lower compensation, physician defections, and, eventually, our demise.

Nalle's strengths

Consumerism

In spite of our failure, we had a number of important strengths. Rising consumerism helped Nalle. Customer service feedback showed high patient satisfaction in the clinical arena. We developed customer and peer satisfaction surveys and provided physicians with the results at least annually. Results were very positive. Physicians were counselled over unfavourable responses, and we observed measurable changes in behaviour. We had complaints, but overwhelmingly they were over the billing process.

Local competition

The local competitive environment between the two health systems also helped. We were able to get competitive managed care contracts. Health plans liked our good patient satisfaction marks. Our managed care performance was competitive for our region, with rates of 160–180 bed days per 1,000. The health plans were playing the three largest providers in the market against one another—the two hospital systems and the clinic. They did not want the hospitals to become too powerful. We enjoyed another advantage in that we admitted to both systems and patients were able to see us regardless of whether their plan moved from one hospital to the other.

High quality medicine

We had excellent physicians who practised high quality medicine. We provided not only high technical quality but also compassionate personal care. We developed systems to provide high quality care with good resource conservation for our HMO patients. The collegial environment, the clinic setting, and the unified medical record allowed us to coordinate care across different specialities. We had an effective contracting strategy that allowed us to leverage our size and independent status into better-than-average contracts. We had delivery sites throughout Mecklenburg County and were well positioned with satellites in all the right places.

Nalle's weaknesses

A disconnect between actions and consequences.

Our weaknesses were subtle but more pervasive. Like many large medical clinics, we suffered from a disconnect between a physician's actions and the consequences of those actions. Compensation was based on total clinical production multiplied by a speciality-specific factor to account for overhead, differences between profitability of different specialities, and the "primary care supplement". The dynamics of the income distribution plan were such that the impact of a physician's performance—whether he or she worked particularly hard or had a more leisurely pace—tended to be spread throughout the entire group.

If physicians felt they were underpaid, for example, they focused on the formula, or what was the "clinic" doing about it, rather looking at the processes, expenses, or productivity of their practice. In contrast, in a solo practice, the impact, whether good or bad, directly affects the individual. Similarly, physicians did not benefit from sacrificing for expense reductions or suffer from excessive expenses.

Mismanaging physician performance

Managing physician performance and process improvement were other casualties. Historically, we had relied upon individual work ethic to [motivate] physician productivity and performance. Unfortunately, we lacked valid feedback mechanisms to help individuals know where they stood compared to their peers and the clinic's needs. No one felt they needed to improve their performance, which blunted the incentive to move to a more uncomfortable, but possibly better "new way". This is "the way we have always done it" was the overwhelming attitude.

Jack Silversin, MD, has described this phenomenon in multi-specialty groups as the "old compact," in which the individual expects entitlement, protection, and autonomy, whereas in the "new compact," the individual needs to feel a sense of ownership, interdependence, customer focus, and delegated decision-making.

Complicated billing process

Increasing numbers of physicians, specialities, and health plans have caused more complexity in preparing bills, filing claims, and collecting money. Each speciality has coding nuances. For example, someone accustomed to coding for a gastroenterologist would not necessarily have the knowledge to properly code for an orthopaedic surgeon. Similarly, each health plan has differences in their pre-certification and claims filing process—and sometimes they don't pay legitimate claims promptly.

Without sophisticated billing systems and dedicated staff to navigate this labyrinth, revenue was lost and patients became frustrated. A driving force in entering into the relationship with PhyCor was the expectation that they could efficiently manage accounts receivable. But we never were able to make the business office perform up to industry standards.

In some ways, the artificial separation of responsibilities into "medical" and "business" made change more difficult. Physicians felt that problems in the business office were purely an administrative function and resisted process change that would improve collections but complicate the flow of patients through the clinic.

Shoot the messenger syndrome

Administration was reluctant to involve physicians in change initiatives because of the "shoot the messenger syndrome." When a problem was pointed out, the response was, "Why hasn't this been fixed before now?" rather than, "How can we solve this?" Business office problems undoubtedly hurt profitability, took a toll on customer satisfaction, and created a vicious cycle. We needed to invest in a computer system for accounts receivable, but we did not feel that we could afford it. Stress and pressure in the business office created a harsh work environment, which led to staff defections, which led to more stress and pressure.

Overhead structure

Our overhead was high when compared to industry benchmarks, particularly the MGMA annual reports on cost. We were unwilling to make the changes necessary to drive down costs and tacitly accepted a somewhat higher cost structure. Support staff salary expense was higher than benchmark comparisons. Capital expenses, such as leases and rent, were also high. We moved into the Randolph Road building in 1995 and fell in love with it. It was spacious, attractive—and expensive. In the mid-90s we opened two satellites in growing areas of town—they quickly became busy but added to the increasing cost structure.

The PhyCor fee was always a burden. But it also had a more insidious effect. As profit margins became tighter and compensation declined, the physicians focused on this fee as the root of all our financial problems, rather than looking at other, more basic, parts of the overall structure.

Attempts to change course

We needed a culture shift to help improve productivity, decrease expenses, and facilitate process improvement. Initially, we set productivity and expense control targets and rewards accordingly. Then we started changing the compensation structure to reflect the economics of each site, on the theory that the physicians were in the best position to manage their production and expenses.

We were evaluating a new computer system to help manage accounts receivable. Many of our collections problems started with registration at the individual sites. We were developing a "front end" process in which all demographic and health plan data was verified before the patient was seen. Historically, the service was rendered, the claim submitted, and the bill fixed on the "back end" if payment was denied.

Our profitability was lagging and most of our primary care competitors had a relationship with one of the hospital systems. We focused on getting help from an outside entity, first PhyCor and then one of the hospitals. In 1998 and 1999, many realised that declining profitability was a big problem and that increased productivity was part of the solution. But gaining significant changes in behaviour would be time consuming and would require one-on-one coaching with the staff. Pursuing a "hospital deal" seemed like a better way to use limited physician management resources.

But despite our efforts, we were running out of time.

Signs of trouble

The sequence of key events began with an unusually weak first quarter in 1998, which had traditionally been our strongest period. By the end of the year, we saw a trend toward lower profitability. We developed an action plan to close two satellites, eliminate unprofitable services, and reduce personnel. In early 1998, PhyCor had infused additional cash, and we opened discussions with one of the hospitals to develop a mutually beneficial relationship that would also help our profitability. As this discussion continued, we delayed implementing our cost savings plan and concentrated on concluding the hospital deal.

Throughout 1999, we felt that a hospital deal was just a "couple of weeks away". The weeks and months of waiting eventually took their toll and we began to see the defections of a few physicians. As they left, we couldn't decrease expenses proportionate to the lost revenue and profitability deteriorated further. In early 2000, we were negotiating with PhyCor to repurchase our assets, which ultimately failed. We had a poor month in the business office in January and a spectacularly poor month in February. The almost non-existent paycheques at the end of March were the straws that broke the camel's back and we experienced massive resignations, sealing the fate of the Nalle Clinic.

■ Jeremiah H. Holleman, Jr., MD, was President of the Nalle Clinic from 1994 until 30 April 2000. He is now practising peripheral vascular surgery at the Sanger Clinic in Charlotte, North Carolina. He can be reached at 704/444-4010 or jholleman@sanger-clinic.com.

Commentary

Dr. Holleman's post-mortem

Irwin Rubin, PhD

EXTERNAL CIRCUMSTANCES beyond anyone's control will often threaten a patient's well being. The same is true for a Patient. To refer to the health care environment, an environment characterised by "turbulence...increased expenses, decreased reimbursements, and more regulatory pressure", which heads Dr. Holleman's list of nails in Nalle's coffin as challenging is, in my view, an important under-statement. Hostile and dis-eased would be more reflective. Providing a Patient needed TLC when, with increasing frequency, human beings in need of care—patients—are being referred to with phrases like revenue bodies and profit centres is well beyond merely a challenge. Add to this the ever increasing threat of malpractice suits and we have a condition where striving to help a Patient stay healthy in such a toxic environment requires leadership of extraordinary courage, foresight, integrity, faith, not to mention skill.

Given that such environmental conditions remain essentially outside of any single organisation's control, two factors become of paramount importance. One has to do with ensuring that how the organisation is reacting to and dealing with uncontrollable external circumstances does not exacerbate that which is already sapping vital energies and resources. External environmental conditions impact large numbers of Patient organisations equally, and yet some seem to survive and adapt to this toxicity.

The other has to do with ensuring that the things that can be controlled are getting the added scrutiny and care they require. To refer back to our patient analogy for a moment, when a sever flu bug is in the air, conscious steps need to be taken to keep our immune systems as strong as possible lest we allow ourselves to become weakened to the point where we succumb to the germs all around us. The tendency health care organisations have to slash the human resource/training and development budget when economic pressures increase is familiar. To invest less in one's "most important assets" when more is being required of them is totally illogical. It would be akin to asking a patient to pinch their nose and wear a thick face mask while taking a treadmill exam.

Both of those factors, and this point is, in my view, of vital importance, focus attention on the issue of HOW. I have absolutely no disagreement with Holleman's list of Lessons Learned. By and large, their focus is on WHAT might have been done to keep the Patient's pulse beating. However, driving any efforts to focus upon and achieve tasks like "pay attention to managing accounts receivable, develop reserves, if possible, and monitor your expense structure carefully, particularly fixed expenses" is the human process—HOW people behave towards and communicate with one another.

I have noted elsewhere[1] that the sum total of all an organisation's day-to-day behavioural interactions is both rooted in and reinforces the organisation's culture. An organisation's culture thus becomes akin to a human being's blood stream. Just as our blood flows through and affects (or infects, as the case may be) every organ in our bodies, so, too, will an organisation's culture flow through and affect every task—every WHAT—the organisation must accomplish. Behaviour and interpersonal communication are to a Patient what blood flow and oxygen are to a patient. Holleman's senses this when he comments: "Our weaknesses were subtle but more pervasive."

Consequently, just as bad blood, vitamin deficient blood, guarantees that a patient's body becomes weakened, so, too, will "bad blood" between individual elements in an organisation guarantee that the Patient's body becomes weakened. And when an organisation's human culture—its fundamental behavioural and communication processes—is weakened, steps must first be taken to care for this human culture before new challenging task can be tackled.

Holleman was absolutely right when he noted: "We needed to change course...to improve productivity, decrease expenses, and facilitate process improvement [through] setting productivity and expense control targets and rewards accordingly...changing compensation structures...evaluating new computer systems to help manage accounts receivable." If he was "right on" what went wrong?

---

[1] Dr. Irwin M. Rubin, PhD, 'Total quality management: care dealers vs. car dealers', *Physician Executive*, September–October 1992, vol. 8, no. 5, pp. 15–20. Dr. Irwin M. Rubin, PhD, *Transforming Organizational Cultures: Simple as ABCs*, available from Temenos, Inc.

The Nalle Clinic appears to have made several very common errors. Looking at Holleman's list of nails in Nalle's coffin, I wonder if they confused a focus on independent symptoms with fundamentally interdependent causes. In the acute phases of the Patient's, the organisation's, threatened demise, addressing this list of nails sequentially may have actually contributed to the ultimate death. Considering a new billing system, for example, which may have improved the economic system and the flow of money may only have served to prolong the agony felt in other sub-systems.

Metabolism of a constant supply of energy is the chemical expression of life. The Nalle Clinic's ultimate collapse came when a prime source of energy—money—for its human components, its staff, dwindled and stopped. But the fact that money is not the sole source of organisational fuel leaves us with some very important questions to ponder. Did the Patient lose its will to live long before the money ran out? Did the metabolic rate fall out of sync earlier? Did the heart start to beat erratically before the economic bleeding became unstoppable?

Life requires proper functioning of all systems, in patients and Patients. Consequently, a critical action for "Attending" leaders of health care organisations is to understand the metabolic rate of their Patient and to keep their fingers on the pulse so they can take action as soon as an anomaly is identified and before it becomes acute.[2]

A second typical pitfall has to do with what needs to be changed when. Of course the Nalle Clinic needed a "culture shift!" Elements of the "condominium" Stage One level of organisational development mindset seem to have begun creeping back into Nalle's culture. [See earlier Commentary: Organisations Have To Grow Up for a review of the Stages of Organisational Growth and Development.] This is the "old compact" set of attitudes to which Silversin refers. (See next Commentary for more detail on this point.)

But the needed shift was at the human level FIRST, not the task level. A poor problem-solving process—the norms and behaviours people are exhibiting as they go about solving problems—must, by definition, yield poor problem-solving outcomes.

Two examples will suffice. The first required the realisation and acceptance of the fact that "the separation of responsibilities into 'medical' and 'business' [not only] made change more difficult" was a belief that violated the fundamental premise that the Nalle Clinic was a

---

[2] Dr. Irwin M. Rubin, Ph.D., "From Boardroom to Treatment Room: Vital Signs of Health", available from Temenos, Inc.

human organism, a Patient. To artificially compartmentalise parts of the whole ran the same risk as allowing us to define a patient with a strong heart as being healthy, in spite of the fact that its liver was failing. With the same ultimate consequence!

Even more disconcerting is the underlying cause of the naiveté of this belief, which Holleman acknowledges when he notes—"little did we realise that there were almost no issues that were either purely practice or business. Rather, every medical decision impacted the business, and every business decision affected the practice of medicine". The fact that the organisation's blood stream, its human culture, touches every element of the whole makes this fact inevitable. The Nalle Clinic reflected a cultural dynamic that is rampant across many health care organisms—a less-than win-win true partnership relationship between physicians and administrators. The separation belief provided a convenient conflict avoidance belief mechanism: each part could blame the others as the cause of the problems without having to take responsibility and accountability for their own actions.

Let me frame the cultural issue as an admittedly rhetorical set of questions. Holleman acknowledges that the interpersonal blood stream running through the Nalle Clinic was being infected by a rampant cultural dynamic, the "shoot the messenger syndrome". This same blood stream carried a strong focus on finding scapegoats versus learning from mistakes: "Why hasn't his been fixed before now? versus "How can we solve this?" If this was the kind of blood flowing through the Patient's communication arteries, what level of quality could we expect with respect to the content outcome of vital task-related decisions; e.g. changing compensation structures…evaluating new computer systems to help manage accounts receivable…developing the absent and needed feedback mechanisms to help individuals where they stood compared to their peers and the clinic's needs?

With the power of 20-20 hindsight, we have to wonder if the Patient might not have had the opportunity to have been better cared for if the diagnosis of the human health of the organisation referred to in the earlier Commentary on 'Organisational cultural change: a self-help programme' had been repeated when it began to show the symptoms of significant dis-ease.

Given the above, we cannot be surprised that previously "high patient satisfaction" began to erode. "Staff defections" rose further eroding an already shaky morale, a nervous and frightened Patient. The ensuing viscous cycle, which Holleman acknowledges finally, took its toll. "The almost non-existent paycheques at the end of March 2000 was the straw that broke the camel's back and [the clinic] experienced massive resignations, sealing the fate of the Patient, the Nalle Clinic"...and hundreds of thousands of patients who had sought its care since 1921.

In perhaps his most poignant comment, Holleman notes that possibly "the only bright part of this tragedy has been to see how the Nalle Clinic physicians continued to serve their patients during the final months, in spite of having been paid nothing".

With such a fundamental commitment to patient care, with such a reflection of what the heart and soul of the entire profession of health care stands for, it is vital that we continue to ponder deeply whether or not the demise of the Nalle Clinic was inevitable.

For myself, personally, I can only conclude that anytime we allow ourselves to treat the Patient with anything less than the highest quality of human care and caring of which we are humanly capable, we end up compromising our ability to deliver the highest quality of patient care of which we are capable.

The real tragedy in the demise of the Nalle Clinic would be the failure of its passing to increase our awareness of and commitment to the Patient's need for TLC as being the true leadership challenge involved in keeping a health care organisation's pulse strongly beating.

Commentary

The tragic dynamic in medical group practices

Mary Jane Kornacki, MS and Jack Silversin DMD, DrPH

Editor's note: Dr. Holleman's autopsy notes, and Dr. Fernandez's notes which follow, painfully point to the inability of the Nalle Clinic to follow its own prescriptions for continued growth and development. While many visible factors contributed to the clinic becoming a non-compliant Patient, a series of fundamental less visible but nonetheless vital deeply rooted physician-held attitudes and beliefs were also operating to contribute to its demise. Based on their extensive experience in leading physicians through change, Dr. Jack Silversin and Ms. Mary Jane Kornacki—to whom Dr. Holleman refers several times—have generously shared some seminal and poignant thoughts on some of these underlying attitudes for us to reflect upon in considering why the Patient did not survive. Dr. Silversin and Ms Kornacki are founding partners of Amicus, a health care consulting firm based in Cambridge, Mass. They are the co-authors of, *Leading Physicians Through Change: How To Achieve and Sustain Results* available from the American College of Physician Executives. For more information about Amicus see www. consultamicus.com

THE HISTORY AND dynamics that led to the failure of the Nalle Clinic are not all that unique. The fraternity model [a Stage I organisation in our terminology] and inability to mature as a business are traits common to many medical group practices. Even if not terminal or in bankruptcy, many groups are incapacitated from effectively changing to meet consumer needs and payer demands thus compromise their future vitality. The slow response to a changed external environment is very often rooted in the beliefs held by physicians. The following myths undermine a group's capacity to change:

- *Myth No. 1*—"It's someone else's job to mind the business—as a doctor, my job is to see patients". This belief has dangerously strong appeal. If it only it were true! Any dichotomy between clinical care and business realities is illusory. When doctors believe they can practise without attending to the financial implications of their work, the dynamic for failure is set in motion. Doctors need to be business literate. In addition, they need to embrace other aspects of the business of running the practice—including their role as the most important determinant of staff morale and commitment. Knowing that doctors prefer providing clinical care to pouring over P and L statements, companies like PhyCor made deals that doctors couldn't resist. The premise that a successful partnership can be built on "We'll take care of business, all you have to do is see patients" has turned out to be false.

- *Myth No. 2*—"All physicians are leaders and, therefore, we don't need to delegate authority to anyone". This belief contributes mightily to the weak model of physician leadership in many group practices. Most physicians expect a leader to be their advocate and representative. Chiefs are seen by others in the department as the one to go to meetings, express the needs of the rest of the department and bring back the resources (then get administration to "leave us alone"). If a chief takes a stand or a board develops a policy, those not included feel little compunction to go along. This accounts for the popularity of town meeting style decision-making. The resistance to delegating authority and living by leaders' decisions slows the rate of change. When a single shareholder can force a board's decision to be re-visited or undone, the group is disabled any kind of rapid response.

- *Myth No. 3*—"Visions are for psychotics". Even though successful businesses of every stripe develop a vision to serve as the bedrock of strategic plans and their competitive advantage, most doctors don't get it. To most physicians, the "V-word" is something to be avoided. Most believe that something as "soft and fuzzy" as vision has limited value. Many would tell you the vision and the group's financial bottom line are one and the same. And, furthermore, that the bottom line is likely to be black when every doctor does his or her personal best making a group-wide vision irrelevant.

  This is a tragic underestimation of two critical ways a shared vision can serve a medical group. First, honest conversation to develop a shared vision ought to get on the table the different opinions and divergent views that group members hold. If the process is superficial the controversies will be papered over and the doctors will be right—the vision is useless. If done well, the visioning process airs issues too often shoved under the rug. If for no other reason, that makes the process a valuable one. Second, the shared vision ought to align resources, priorities, and decisions about what strategies to pursue and which to drop. It should help leaders develop parameters for unacceptable behaviour and help individual doctors decide if they want to "get off the bus". Instead of touchy-feely shared vision needs to be a powerful and useful lever for gaining commitment and moving a group into the future.

- *Myth No. 4*—"As a doctor, I'm entitled to autonomy, security, and status". Not challenging this belief—in light of new imperatives—is the undoing of many medical groups. The traditional compact—or psychological contract—held that once doctors joined a practice they would enjoy clinical autonomy, be protected from market forces and enjoy privileges other staff did not (e.g. best parking spaces, broad definition of acceptable behaviour). These expectations are developed in the physician's training and socialisation. In the past, these could be honoured at no risk or cost to the group. Today however, they are impediments to the imperatives to be patient-centred, document quality care, and ensure safety. Without an adjustment in physicians' basic expectations, the change initiatives groups undertake are difficult to sustain. The groups with the best shot at long-term health are surfacing unstated expectations and, with physicians, re-writing their compact.

Actions to thrive

The capacity to change in many medical practices is dangerously inadequate. The inability to move as quickly inside as forces on the outside are moving results from unwillingness to empower leaders, lack of deeply shared vision, outdated expectations, and lack of working knowledge of financial matters. When it's "change or die", it's too late to have the conversations that build change capacity. The difference between organisational health and failure is de-bunking the myths, facing reality and getting good at change before the wolf shows up at the door.

Autopsy comments

Ray Fernandez, MD

Editor's note: In his last chart entry to the first edition of *My Pulse*, Dr. Fernandez's prognosis for the Patient's health was quite optimistic: "The patient that was last in intensive care and had to be referred out to a specialist is now back in full health. There is a sense of pride that now we are meeting certain goals that had to be met. That accomplishment is much more important than bickering about which administration is accomplishing it." At the same time, when the Clinic decided to reduce the Medical Director's role from a full time job to a 65 percent, Dr. Fernandez had to 'vigorously' argue with his colleagues to reverse their decision: "It seemed to me like a patient who was over an acute illness and no longer in pain, jumping to the conclusion that they didn't need as much medical care...I pointed out that it was premature to declare victory, that in spite of the essential support that PhyCor offered, it would be a step backward to diminish the time, knowledge, energy, and commitment to the Clinic to promoting its own internal systems in growing up."

And, as we've already seen from Dr Holleman's comments, in spite of the bringing on board of the new "specialist"—PhyCor—victory celebrations were indeed premature. The Nalle Clinic became a Patient who had rallied from their original serious illness to the restoration of apparent good health only to later find that a terminal illness had once again begun to manifest itself. Dr. Fernandez's retrospective comments (since he himself, as we shall see, left the Nalle Clinic a few years before its demise) follow below.

FOR THE FIRST 5 years of our new partnership, there was personalised attention given by the young PhyCor management team to the Nalle Clinic. This commitment and attention to detail resulted in significant progress. Profitability had been restored to the clinic. It began a period of exciting growth. It acquired several primary care practices even though it had to "out-bid" several hospitals suitors to acquire these very prestigious practices. New physicians were recruited and the clinic size grew to 140 physicians. New satellite locations were built around the city and a new 225,000 square foot home facility was constructed. New computer software linked all the physicians with a communication system that was the envy of other providers and also provided the ability to transmit medical information about shared patients quickly and efficiently.

The prestige of the clinic continued to grow. This new model of an integrated unit between the business management folks at PhyCor and the local physicians seemed to offer much promise. Groups from around the country came to study our success and to attempt to mimic it. The industry of physician practice management companies, like PhyCor, prospered and did extremely well initially on the stock market. The potential of sound management principles being applied to medical practices seemed to represent the logical extension of tried and true techniques taught at the nation's finest business schools.

However, hidden under this veneer of success was a Patient who continued to consume more of its own energies than what it could replace. The managerial expertise offered by PhyCor turned out to provide less of an unshakeable foundation against the vagrancies of an ever increasingly uncertain and turbulent health care environment than had been hoped for, or realised in the earlier honeymoon period. The needs for continued growth required by the stock market could not be sustained. Eventually the public-captive markets lost their interest in this new "industry" and redirected capital to the more glitzy industries associated with the dotcom logo.

Why did the honeymoon end, and why in death versus just divorce? With 20-20 hindsight, several contributing factors are painfully clear. Firstly, PhyCor did not offer any fundamental change in the way health care was delivered. There was no magic in the business principles that it brought to the table, and its ability to deliver better than average business results never could be realised. The initial increase in confidence that the doctors experienced was not sustained. For example, the percentage of profits that had to be funnelled to PhyCor's home office in Nashville turned out to be more than the valued benefits brought to the table. So, after several years, it began to be apparent that the "magic" and the infused confidence that PhyCor brought in 1990 was not sufficient to continue meeting true success of the clinic as an operating entity. Medical care was never sacrificed and the clinic continued to enjoy its reputation as a quality provider of excellent physicians. However, the physicians started to experience a similar increasing overhead of the kind that had led them to seek a relationship with PhyCor in the first place.

As the Nalle Clinic's physicians shared their business experiences with their colleagues in other practices, they came to realise that their performance as a business entity was actually inferior to other practices that did not invest in the overhead items that the clinic thought to be necessary to support its size. This realisation translated into a loss of confidence in the leaders of the clinic, where leaders were defined generally as anyone who was elected to serve on the board.

Physicians have always been good about electing someone that they trust to a position of authority. But, whenever anything goes wrong (regardless of whether or not the events might be out of anyone's control) they start to criticise the abilities of someone whom they respected. Now the leadership of the board was half lay-businessmen appointed by PhyCor. They made even easier targets for criticism since they were "not one of us" (meaning a physician in the trenches).

Although physicians could see many specific things that needed to be changed, no one wanted to have their own pet projects diminished. Any board member who might suggest closing a satellite or closing a new programme would be wrongly criticised and not get support from anyone else. Thus the stakes, even obvious ones that everyone could identify, would rarely get reversed. It seemed that, like the government, once a programme started, it never ended even though it might not have fulfilled its intentions.

So, by 1998, it became apparent that the Nalle Clinic was still not being nearly as successful as a business entity as it was as a care giving entity. The continuing pride in its ability to deliver health care services was a bit of hubris that prevented it from addressing the problem as a business entity. Besides, PhyCor could always be blamed for this since they represented the "great business men" who would make the "tough business decisions".

The consequences of these conditions were becoming painfully clear to a group of 140 physicians who were seeing the corporation that they owned continue to deteriorate and show less profitability with each passing year. Its end product of delivering quality health care to a large number of patients disguised the fact that it was consuming its own needed resources to do this. Like the loyal subjects of the emperor who had no clothes, the physicians individually realised that they were digging a deeper hole for themselves, but simply could not empower themselves collectively to reverse the trend.

The crisis in confidence in the leaders escalated to the point that, by the late 1990s, very few people were willing to even run for positions on the board of directors. With PhyCor's agreement, seeking a partner from one of the local hospitals seemed to represent the only way that survival might be guaranteed. So, just as the union with PhyCor in 1990 produced the "blood transfusion" that the Patient needed to temporarily restore health, a similar type of therapy was now being sought again.

Incredibly, the chosen hospital partner that the clinic worked with for almost a year could not deliver on its promise of assistance. But by then the die had been cast and failure seemed more imminent. There arose a certain amount of in-fighting and factionism amongst the clinic leaders. An outright challenge resulted over who should direct the board and who should continue as the chief physician executive.

It was during these crises that I personally decided to leave the clinic. While I felt very torn about this decision, I deeply believed that doing so might be best for my own career and, at the same time, might help the clinic come to grips with the need to rally behind a single leader. So, in November of 1999 I left the Nalle Clinic to accept a new leadership position in another organisation in another state.

PhyCor's ability to tap into appropriate captive markets continued to diminish rapidly and they very soon thereafter went into bankruptcy. The Nalle Clinic decided that the best decision to take was also to dissolve. Thus the entity that had delivered care to this community in a professional way for over 75 years decided to close its doors.

Even with the benefit of time and distance, I find myself mulling over a host of "What ifs?" Could the organisation, the Patient, have been saved by recall to another specialist? Would the Patient have tolerated it and accepted a referral? What could have been done differently? For the last four years of organisational life, it was clear that some things absolutely needed to be done from a business perspective. Closing satellites, taking the tough step of removing several less productive physicians, not continuing to make capital investments when the necessary capital was not available, and a better choice of a hospital partner could all have contributed mightily to a Patient recovering.

But the underlying illness that created many of the "symptoms" noted by the Patient required a stronger governance mechanism. Physicians in this group, as in many others, did not demand an acceptable level of performance from their leaders. They did not address any of the expectations that they had. Consequently, systematically evaluating their leaders became impossible. Rewarding good performance and correcting unacceptable performance became academic.

There is also a sinister lack of directness between the governed and the governing. Physicians who were only too happy to pontificate about all of the obvious problems in the doctors' lunchroom, for some reason, will not take the time to cultivate the same sermon in the boardroom. The physicians concern over their patients and their willingness to do anything to help their patient, in other words, does not seem to extend to their own organisation. Furthermore the physicians are not willing to make the required business decisions to allow their organisation to be a healthy economic entity. Physicians confuse elements of their own comfort (like hiring a new partner to share calls) with tough economic modelling. And the experience at the Nalle Clinic was based on the erroneous belief that simply hiring an outside entity (the PhyCor businessmen) would automatically produce results. Being employed by a businessman is quite different than being a partner in a business, and PhyCor never realised that distinction until it was too late.

Separate from these more clinical "chart-like" entries, I am also left with a host of personal reflections. I made a personal decision to leave the Nalle Clinic at a time of maximum stress for the Patient. The obstetrician who decides to take a long-scheduled family vacation at a time that one of his/her patients is due knows that he is not going to be available for his patient at a time of maximum need. The physician who signs out for his weekend off to his partner only to return on a Monday morning to visit his desperately ill patient in the ICU, and find out the patient expired, feels an element of guilt.

The reality is that the doctor probably could have done nothing better for the patient than the care that they received in his absence. But he and the patient would probably have both felt more comfortable had the death occurred on his watch. That's the only way that he might really know that he "certainly did everything he could" for his patient.

Most physician clinics in partnerships go through a natural process of birth, growth, maturation, and extinction like the human organism. Organisations also can have finite life spans. History teaches us that that is the case. But it's different when studied in the abstract and commented on in general terms. It's different when the patient is someone who is a close family member and whose loss we feel personally.

Consequently, seeing the Nalle Clinic dissolve only after I had left to assume a different position is a most difficult task for me personally. I wish I had been a louder voice and cried out earlier, louder, and longer what needed to be done. Because then it could have been done, the Patient might have survived.

But that might only be wishful thinking for it certainly does presume that the Patient would have listened to any of my advice or my personal experience.

A final commentary

Irwin Rubin, PhD

I**N ADDITION TO** being my co-author, Dr. Fernandez and I have been close friends and colleagues ever since we first met over two decades ago. Consequently, I found myself flooded by a host of reactions to his most recent "chart entries", emanating both from my mind and my heart. So I feel a deep need to begin with a personal reflection first.

The pain of the death of something very near and dear to him—in spite of the distance afforded by time and his new job [and his frequent use of the word "it" in referring to the Nalle Clinic, in sharp contrast to the more frequent reference to words like "we" and "us" in the first edition]—clearly persists. The "guilt" of having had one's patient pass away while taking a much needed weekends rest from call, or the feeling of not having done one's best—"I wish I had been a louder voice and cried out earlier, louder, and longer what needed to be done."—are feelings all physicians can understand. Their roots are the very values and ideals, which brought them to the profession in the first place— to serve their fellow human beings.

Healing from deaths of any kind, be they of single loved ones, or organisations we'd come to love, is a process that knows its own pace. I can only hope that allowing himself to stir up many of these feelings within his own soul, and sharing them with others, has helped a dear friend's heart heal a bit more as well.

Dr. Fernandez's commentary points to several other areas where, because vital healing clearly defined as being essential in the first edition of *My Pulse* did not take place, that the Patient was left in a weakened state. Steps that were clearly indicated as possible "blood transfusion" measures, like "closing satellites, taking the tough step of removing several less productive physicians, not continuing to make capital investments when the necessary capital was not available, and a better choice of a hospital partner could all have contributed mightily to a Patient recovering" simply did not come to pass.

When an individual patient exhibits similar behaviours—eating foods known to worsen a deteriorating heart condition or smoking cigarettes known to weaken their deteriorating lungs—we shake our heads in disbelief. Such is the power of denial, or as Dr. Fernandez labelled it, "a bit of hubris that prevented…addressing…problem[s] as a business entity." When an individual patient exhibits the same behaviours but expects different consequences we label it insanity. It is no more sane, no less "incredible", to see that "the chosen hospital" —the second blood transfusion, the first being the failing union with PhyCor—"could not deliver on its promise of assistance".

While there are undoubtedly many factors that would cause any "blood transfusion" to fail, it is important that we zoom our post-mortem lens in on those that the Patient could have potentially controlled. Those that were also a part of its original "prescriptions" for moving from a Stage One Fraternity to a Stage Two business organisation, as a necessary prerequisite to becoming a Stage Three organisation in constant search of excellence. And the most significant element within any individual patient's control—and, therefore within any Patient's control—is how it chooses to respond to, deal with, and process the threats to its health and well-being life brings before it. In a patient, this constellation of factors is our personality. In a Patient, it is the culture of the organisation, which is itself, the consequences of the day-to-day choices people make about how to behave towards one another.[1]

All of the critically important content decisions the Nalle Clinic had to make—and those it avoided making—were being 'infected' by the culture of the organisation, by the behavioural processes emanating from its culture. And what do both Dr. Holleman and Dr. Fernandez reinforce about the human health and well being of the nature of that culture? A few examples will suffice.

As reported earlier in this book, the original "x-ray" reading of the survey taken of the clinic back in the mid-1980s pointed clearly to a blame-oriented we-they culture. In terms of this characteristic Stage One attitude, the Patient did not experience any fundamental shift. All that changed were the targets—the membership of the we-they factions:[2]

---

[1] Dr. Irwin M. Rubin, PhD, 'Total quality management: care dealers vs. car dealers', *Physician Executive*, September–October 1992, vol. 8, no. 5, pp. 15–20. Dr Irwin M. Rubin, PhD, *Transforming Organizational Cultures: Simple as ABCs*, available from Temenos, Inc.
[2] Dr. Irwin M. Rubin, PhD, 'Intergroup competition: an organization cancer', *Physician Executive*, March–April 1988, pp. 12–17.

- "Now the leadership of the board was half lay-businessmen appointed by PhyCor. They made even easier targets for criticism since they were 'not one of us' (meaning a physician in the trenches)."
- "Besides PhyCor could always be blamed for this since they represented the 'great businessmen' who would make the 'tough business decisions'."
- "There arose a certain amount of in-fighting and factionalism amongst the clinic leaders. An outright challenge resulted over who should direct the board and who should continue as the chief physician executive."

A Stage One Fraternity heart will reject "blood transfusions" emanating from Stage Two Business mindsets, unless a fundamental distinction is recognised and embraced because, as Dr. Fernandez notes, "being employed by a businessman is quite different than being a partner in a business, and that distinction was never realised by PhyCor until it was too late." I would add that the physicians at the Nalle Clinic failed to make the same distinction. Else how could they justify a series of patterns familiar across much of the entire profession of medicine:

- "Being only too happy to pontificate about all of the obvious problems in the doctors' lunchroom, [but] for some reason, [they] will not take the time to cultivate the same sermon in the boardroom. The physicians' concern over their patients and their willingness to do anything to help their patient, in other words, does not seem to extend to their own organisation."
- "A sinister lack of directness."
- "Taking the tough step of removing several less productive physicians."
- "Physicians...did not demand an acceptable level of performance from their leaders. They did not address any of the expectations that they had. Consequently, systematically evaluating their leaders became impossible. [In contrast to the ever-present behind-the-back evaluations that are rampant in the Doctors' dining rooms.] Rewarding good performance and correcting unacceptable performance became academic."

I have no disagreement with Dr. Fernandez's observation that "the underlying illness that created many of the 'symptoms' noted by the Patient point to the need for a stronger governance mechanism". Indeed, such a stronger governance mechanism [a prescription the

Patient agreed was vital ten years earlier] could have added impetus to
the need for the Nalle Clinic's 140 physicians—"who individually
realised that they were digging a deeper hole for themselves"—to stop
acting like "the loyal subjects of the emperor who had no clothes" so
they could "empower *themselves* collectively to reverse the trend".

The emphasis in the above quote was not in Dr. Fernandez's original
reflections. I do so here because I believe it contains a painful reminder
of the same leadership challenge originally laid before the feet of the
Nalle Clinic—and by unavoidable implication, the entire professions of
medicine and health care. A challenge, which if we do not learn and
embrace its implications, will mean that the Nalle Clinic will have died
in vain.

In the context of the post-mortem observations made by both Drs.
Holleman and Fernandez, the trend to which I am referring has to do
with a lethal—to both patients and Patients—artificial distinction. Dr.
Holleman put it this way: "In some ways, the artificial separation of
responsibilities into 'medical' and 'business' made change more difficult."
Dr. Fernandez's way of framing the same issue was to observe: "So,
after several years, it began to be apparent that the 'magic' and the
infused confidence that PhyCor brought in 1990 was not sufficient to
continue meeting true success of the clinic as an operating entity. [But]
medical care was never sacrificed and the clinic continued to enjoy its
reputation as a quality provider of excellent physicians."

A Patient organisation, a care-giving entity [a care dealership in contrast to car dealerships, as I have referred to them elsewhere[3]], is in the
business of providing health care. The product being offered is curing
and healing, both of which are known to be enhanced by TLC, tender
love and care.[4] There is no distinction between being a business and
delivering quality health care: it IS the business of the business. And we
need managerial and leadership paradigms that acknowledge this
unique oneness, not ones that strive to force car dealership models onto
care dealership businesses.

These Patients, like any other patients, cannot survive without oxygen and healthy blood, without sufficient economic resources. And,
these Patients, like any other patients, require the highest quality of

[3] Dr. Irwin M. Rubin, PhD, 'Total quality management: care dealers vs. car dealers',
Physician Executive, September–October 1992, vol. 8, no. 5, pp. 15–20.
[4] Dr. Irwin M. Rubin, PhD, 'Interpersonal economics: how the 'soft stuff' affects hard
bottom lines', *Health Forum Journal*, September–October 1999, pp. 42–44. Dr. Irwin M.
Rubin, PhD, 'Patient safety and managerial malpractice: what's the connection?' available
from Temenos, Inc.

humane care of which we are humanly capable when they fall ill. So, at the risk of trivialising, the real lessons to be learned from the demise of the Nalle Clinic are—in my humble opinion—quite simple to articulate.

The entire profession/business of medicine must embrace the documented premise that the quality of caring the Patient receives will, ultimately, determine its ability to continue to deliver quality patient care. ["Medical care was never sacrificed and the clinic continued to enjoy its reputation as a quality provider of excellent physicians until the Nalle Clinic decided that the best decision to take was to dissolve." ...to die.]

However, if embracing this premise only serves to inspire physicians to "empower *themselves* collectively"—to "First heal themselves."—we will still have missed the ultimate goal. For such a step will only serve to ensure that more Stage One Fraternity organisations survive to become viable Stage Two Business organisations. Its primary motivation will be defensive and extrinsic in nature—"We've got to survive."

The transformation to Stage Three organisations in search of excellence will only be fuelled by motivations that are primarily offensive and intrinsic in nature: "It is the only way to deliver on our fiduciary responsibility, our Hippocratic Oath." For the transformation to Stage Three can only occur when a true win-win partnership is forged between physician and non-physician health providers, between those in the business of providing care to patients and those in the business of providing care to Patients.

The demise of the Nalle Clinic will, hopefully, make us realise that there can be no more pressing leadership challenge that faces the business of health care.

Bibliography

Berwick, Donald. "Measuring Health Care Quality". *Pediatrics in Review*, 10(1), (July 1988), 16.

Curry, Wesley. "Looking Ahead". *Physician Executive*, 16(1), (January–February 1990), 4.

Delbecq, André L., and Sandra L. Gill. "Justice as a Prelude to Teamwork in Medical Centers". *HCM Review*, Winter, 1985, 45–51.

Erikson, Erik. *Childhood and Society*, Second Edition. New York: W.W. Norton & Company, Inc., 1964.

Fernandez, Charles Raymond. "Personal Managerial Evolution in a Multispecialty Clinic". *Roads to Medical Management*, ed. Wesley Curry. Tampa: AAMD, 1988, 74–77.

Flower, Joe. "The Role of the Leader". *Healthcare Forum Journal*, (May/June 1990), 30–34.

French, John R. P., Jr., and Bertram Raven. "The Bases of Social Power", in *Group Dynamics: Research and Theory*, Third Edition, ed. Dorwin Cartwright and Alvin Zander. New York: Harper & Row, 1968, 263–268. Originally published in *Studies in Social Power*. D. Cartwright, ed. Ann Arbor, Mich.: Institute for Social Research, 1959.

Friedman, Emily. "The Perils of Detachment". *Healthcare Forum Journal*, March/April 1990, 9–10.

Gardner, John. *Recovery of Confidence*. New York: W.W. Norton & Company, Inc., 1970, 29–30.

Gibbs, Nancy. "Sick and Tired". *Time*, 31 July 1989, 48–53.

Holleman, Jeremiah, "The Demise of the Nalle Clinic", *The Physician Executive*, January– February 2001, 26–31.

Naisbitt, John. *Megatrends: Ten New Directions Transforming Our Lives*. New York: Warner Books, 1982.

Peters, Thomas J., and Robert H. Waterman, Jr. *In Search of Excellence*. New York: Harper & Row, 1982, 318–325.

Press, Irwin. "The Predisposition to File Claims: The Patient's Perspective". *Law, Medicine & Health Care*, (April 1984), 53–62.

Rubin, Irwin. "Organizations Have to Grow Up". *Physician Executive*, 13(2) (March–April 1987), 2–6.

Rubin, Irwin. "Managing Fear and Its Effects on the Quality of Care". Temenos®, Inc., USA, 1990.

Rubin, Irwin. "Transforming Organizational Cultures: Simple as ABCs". Temenos®, Inc., USA.

Rubin, Irwin. "From Boardroom to Treatment Room: Vital Signs of Health". Temenos®, Inc., USA.

Rubin, Irwin. "Intergroup competition: an organization cancer", *Physician Executive*, March–April 1988, 12–17.

Rubin, Irwin. "Total quality management: care dealers vs. car dealers", *Physician Executive*, 8(5), (Sept.–Oct. 1992), 15–20.

Rubin, Irwin. "Interpersonal economics: how the 'soft stuff' affects hard bottom lines", *Health Forum Journal* (Sept.–Oct. 1999), 42–44.

Rubin, Irwin. "Patient safety and managerial malpractice: what's the connection?". Temenos®, Inc., USA.

Rubin, Irwin, and Robert Inguagiato. "Behavioral Quality Assurance: A Transforming Experience". *Physician Executive*, 16(5), (Sept.–Oct. 1990), 30–33.

Schutte, James E. "An Impaired Doctor Cost his Colleagues $5 Million". *Medical Economics*, (4 June 1990), 45–50.

Silver, Henry K., MD, and Anita Duhl Glicken, MSW. "Medical Student Abuse: Incidence, Severity, and Significance". *JAMA*, 263(4), (26 January 1990), 527–537.

Made in the USA
Middletown, DE
05 January 2022